Sovereigns, and Double whites

Fruit and flower pioneers of the Tamar Valley

Photographs
Ted Giffords

Text
Joanna Lewis

First published in 2004
by the Tamar Valley AONB Service
Cotehele Quay, Cotehele, St Dominick
Nr. Saltash, Cornwall PL12 6TA
(www.tamarvalley.org.uk)

Further copies are available from the publishers.

ISBN 1-85522-905-6

Designed and typeset by:
Graphic Words, Peter Tavy, Devon
Tel. +44 (0) 1822 810511

Printing and binding:
MJC Print, Plympton, Devon
Tel. +44 (0) 1752 308418

Front cover: Alan and Lucy Langsford, with tools
including a sclum and joey (funnel), Bere Alston
Back cover: Double Whites

Dedicated to the late Freda Brown,
Bill Evans, John Friendship,
Freddie May and Ronnie Wilcocks

Produced with support from the

Local Heritage *initiative*

Contents

Preface...v
Maps...vi-vii
Introduction.. 1

The Beginning of the Horticultural
Revolution: James Walter Lawry..................... 6

St Dominick Parish, Cornwall
    Olive Lawry.. 14
    George and Freda Brown........................... 16
    Veale Family.. 18
    Natalie Allen... 20
    Terry and Vivian Rogers.........................22
    Joyce and Alan Rickard............................ 24
    Courtney Vanstone.................................... 26
    Nigel and Wendy Hunn............................ 28
    Roy Clarke.. 30
    Joe Collins.. 32
    Mary Martin and Virginia Spiers..............36
    Brian Johns..38
    Norma Chapman.. 40
    Geoffrey and Sylvia Mason...................... 42
    Pop Courtis.. 44
    Albert Wills.. 46

Calstock Parish, Cornwall
    John Lanyon... 50
    Martin Crowell.. 52
    Vivian Nelson.. 54
    Mrs Jope.. 56
    Douglas Davy... 58
    Ruth Wilcocks... 60
    Brian and Mim Stephens........................... 64
    Dulcie Stephens... 66
    King Family...68
    Alec Scoble...70
    Mike Venning.. 72
    Norman Trewartha......................................76
    Alan Elias.. 78
    John Trebilcock... 80
    Maud Maddock...82

Pillaton Parish, Cornwall
    Agnes and Ronnie Wilcocks...................... 86
    Richard Harnett... 88

Botus Fleming Parish, Cornwall
    Ernest Townsend..92
    Elaine Nicholls.. 94
    Arthur Blatchford...................................... 96
    Peggy Whale.. 98
    Edgar Doney... 100
    Dorothy Cloake... 102

Bickleigh Parish, Devon
John and Gladys Pethick.........................106
Ron Luke..108
Keith Langman......................................110

Landulph Parish, Cornwall
Amy Cloake.. 114
Fred Billing... 116
Mike Pollock... 118
David Goodchild.................................... 120
Mary Clark.. 122
Rose and Neil Cradick............................ 124
Louis Barrett... 126
Michael and Martin Braund..................... 128
Bill Evans... 130
Peter and Fay du Plessis......................... 132
Barry Richards....................................... 134

Buckland Monachorum Parish, Devon
Peter Argles.. 138

Bere Ferrers Parish, Devon
Alan and Lucy Langsford........................ 142
Sampson and Martin Channon................. 144
Schuttkacker Family............................... 146
Pauline Eick.. 150
Douglas and Paddy Richards................... 152
Peter Brixey.. 154
Woollcombe Family................................ 156

Stan Sherrell... 158
Harold and Arthur Stephens.................... 160
The Doidge Sisters (Vera Jackson
and Kathleen Webber)........................... 162
Septimus Jackson................................... 164
Nigel Timpson....................................... 166
Norman Grills.. 168
Iris Snell.. 170
John Snell... 172

Harvesting Memories.............................. 175

Glossary... 176

Appendices
Some of the Fruit and Flowers grown..... 191
The Experimental Stations...................... 197
Advisors, Firms and Organisations......... 198
Flower Shows..200
Celebrations.. 201

Bibliography..202

Acknowledgements................................ 204

Index...205

CD Track List...208

Preface
Virginia Spiers

In 1961, when I mapped the market gardens of St. Dominic for geography A Level, land at Boetheric, Burraton and Halton Quay was still intensively cultivated with an intricate patchwork of strawberries, daffodils, anemones, iris, double whites, vegetables, rhubarb and pittosporum. On the earliest, very steep ground at Brentswood and Cleave (across the Cotehele millstream) tilling and weeding were done almost entirely with hand-tools. To avoid soil erosion some of the crops were planted diagonally across slopes and slumped earth was scooped and winched uphill.

Bunches of daffodils were forced open in kitchens and packing sheds, packed in boxes and sent mainly upcountry via Saltash station at an average rail cost of 12 to 15 shillings per cwt. Outdoor strawberries, ready in early June, were picked into half-pound punnets, which had recently superceded the older style two pound chip baskets, and sent away in crates of 24, or sold locally. Old cherry trees planted by earlier generations produced occasional bumper crops but the Trenances' beautiful orchards of plums underplanted with ornatus narcissi, overlooking the river and vividly remembered by my parents' and grandparents' generations were gone.

Today, most of the Tamar Valley's productive plots are amalgamated with grass and arable fields and the steepest have reverted to woodland. Increasingly, fruit, vegetables and flowers are imported from abroad and the once self-sufficient, versatile and skilled growers are mostly retired or semi-retired with no successors. Their characterful and dignified portraits together with those of a few remaining horticulturists and highly specialised producers, photographed by Ted Giffords are reproduced in this book.

The introduction and appendices give background and associated facts and an intriguing glossary explains colloquialisms such as coose, opes, point stuff, vizgies and drawing up cars. Joanna Lewis and Kayleigh Milden have sensitively coaxed from growers reminiscences of dedicated relentlessly hardworking lives and the collection of anecdotes brings the almost defunct industry to life. We can imagine pickers singing to each other across the river, the toddler "bunching leaves" beside her mother, sense the "raw terrible" itch of daffodil rash, the "smell of fruit down the valley" and the overpowering perfume of double whites en masse. It is a poignant testament to the pride taken in work in the days when "every little plot was cultivated".

Map 1: Location of the Tamar Valley

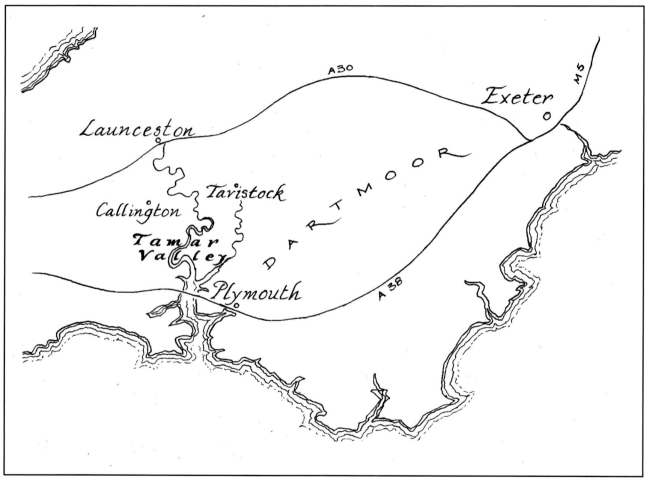

(Ian Pethers)

Map 2: The Tamar Valley

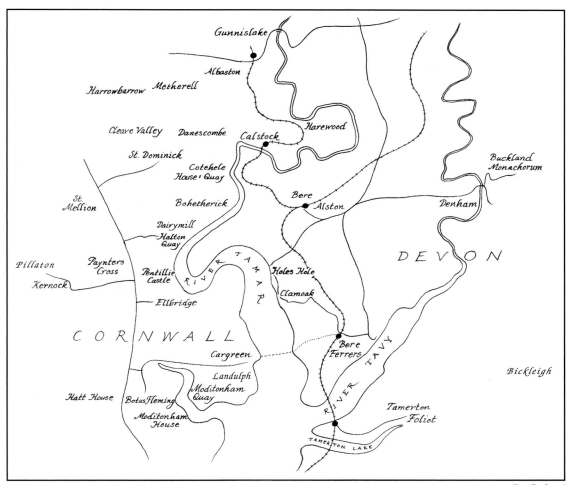

(Ian Pethers)

Introduction

The Tamar Valley has long marked the old Celtic boundary between England and Cornwall. Nowadays the area is a protected landscape, hidden, tranquil and beautiful, the river mostly used for pleasure and recreation. However, like many landscapes in Britain, there are many secrets and stories hidden within the farms and woodlands of the Tamar Valley.

For centuries the Tamar river was the lifeblood of the area, enabling communication, producing food and providing power for a once highly industrialised mining landscape. For a brief period of twenty years in the mid nineteenth century the Tamar Valley became the copper centre of England, the river crowded with shipping carrying ore to be smelted in South Wales. However by 1868 the largest mine, Devon Great Consols, was nearly exhausted and metal prices slumped putting hundreds of families out of work. Arsenic refining took over but in turn was abandoned. By the 1930s mining was dead leaving a strange and dramatic landscape of waste tips and ruinous buildings half hidden in lush woodland and intricately mixed with villages, farms, riverside quays and market gardens.

Ivy Bennett, Champernownes, 1952
Facing page: East Down, St Dominick, 1956
(Nigel Hunn)

1

The Congdon family at Dairymill Farm, carrying strings of round strawberry punnets, 1877 (Brenda Johns)

Alongside mining the valley was famed for its cherry and apple orchards and until recently supported a huge but very concentrated market gardening industry. The market gardens were known as "gardens" and were nearly all family-run, generally of only three to four acres and on sheltered south-facing slopes. The tidal river helped reduce frost and the steep valleys sheltered the holdings from the south west wind. For almost a hundred years the valley was the "earliest" strawberry growing area in the country: "used to be if you had early strawberries you could make money, good money".

Until mechanisation in the 1950s they were largely worked by hand. "We didn't get backache on the hills because you weren't bending over all the time like you would on flat ground." Special tools were made to work the slopes such as the Tamar Valley dibber.

In the 1900s as disease became rampant amongst the fruit plantations the growers started to cultivate daffodils on a vast scale. The indigenous *Tamar Double White* became the valley's most famous flower: "I never met anyone who didn't like *Double Whites* - they were head and shoulders above other narcissus. The boxes were always lined with blue paper, it really set them off". Many of the old varieties still flower in hedges and in odd corners where cultivation has long been abandoned.

Looking around the valley it is at first hard to see evidence of this once thriving economy, but given a few clues and pointers a secret landscape can be quickly revealed. Today it is hard to comprehend that this landscape, mostly shrouded in scrub and woodland on the steep valley sides, supported an industry of eight to ten thousand people at the height of the season in the 1950s, more than the entire population today. Indeed in the early 1950s it was said that "a message from a grower on the Devon side of the valley at Rumleigh could be passed over the hedges and across the River Tamar to another grower in Cargreen."

This was the industry's last peak as from then on the numbers began to melt rapidly away. By 1971 there were about 250 viable holdings; in 1979 there were 140 growers left, many of the extreme slopes so characteristic of the industry having gone out of cultivation. Today there are perhaps thirty growers, some of whom are included in this book. "It used to be there was a job for everyone in the valley." Within living memory the industry has all but vanished and much of its footprint has disappeared. Despite this it has left an indelible impact on the landscape and culture of the area.

The Rickards using a plough attached to an earth car at Brentswood (Ellbridge)

In 2001 a project was established to uncover the landscape of market gardening in the Tamar Valley. This book is an offshoot of that project. The work was initiated by the Tamar Valley Service and has been completed in partnership with the Cornwall County Council Historic Environment Unit, the National Trust at Cotehele and the Institute of Cornish Studies and funded by the Local Heritage Initiative and the Countryside Agency.

The research used a combination of methods such as transferring historic documents, maps and aerial photographs onto computers, surveys of the landscape and archival searches. Natalie Allen's books describing the rich social and horticultural history through the reminiscences of St Dominick villagers initially inspired us to want to photograph some of those involved and the chance appearance of photographer Ted Giffords made this possible. This book includes photographs of many of our informants, some of whom were or are directly involved as growers and others with long family traditions in the industry. Part of their oral history was also recorded.

These stories and photographs are arranged by parish. The market gardening industry was concentrated in six parishes although it spilled out into those bordering them such as Stoke Climsland. On the Cornish side these were St Dominick, Calstock, Botus Fleming and Landulph and on the Devon side Bere Ferrers and to a lesser extent Bickleigh. We begin with St Dominick where the strawberry rush began. Through the photographs on the following pages, the shared memories and by listening to some of the voices on the CD, it is hoped that part of this "Sleeping Beauty" of a landscape will be revealed.

The Beginning of the Horticultural Revolution: James Walter Lawry
(1840 - 1931)

For hundreds of years there had been a horticultural industry in the Tamar Valley selling produce to local markets. However it was not until the last quarter of the nineteenth century that this exploded into a full blown strawberry rush based on selling early fruit to up-country markets. It was the arrival of the Great Western Railway, which reached Plymouth in 1849, bridging the Tamar to Saltash in 1859, coupled with the growing pool of unemployed mining labour that made this horticultural revolution possible. The key to the industry's success was the speed with which the railway delivered perishable fruit to distant markets, within twenty-four hours of being picked.

James Walter Lawry, the son of a tenant farmer in Bohetherick, St Dominick, born on 14 April 1840 was the catalyst in transforming the local industry into "the earliest outdoor strawberry growing region in England" which it remained for almost a hundred years. In 1862 at the age of twenty-two James Lawry visited the Crystal Palace in London and recorded:

"After seeing the show, having heard of Covent Garden Market, my friend and self determined that we would rise early and visit this renowned market whilst yet business was in progress. It was early in June and to my surprise, I found that there were no out-of-door grown strawberries offered, whilst the crop at home was nearly finished before we left. On enquiring the price of the hot house fruit offered, I was staggered at the difference from that we had been receiving at Devonport.

"I got into conversation with a salesman named Israel, and explained that I had hailed from Cornwall and was a grower of strawberries which were now practically finished, although if he would undertake the sale I would write the people at home and get them to forward a small quantity as an experiment. He promised to do his best, and I made the venture…"

In the following year 1863: "The first fruit gathered was duly despatched to Mr. Israel, and being the only out-of-door grown strawberries in the Market, made what to me was an astonishing price, viz 2s 6d per lb. At that time the price made at Devonport was only 6d per lb. Of course I sent all I had to Mr. Israel and seeing that there were other growers sending to Devonport I offered to give the price making there (so saving market costs), and obtained large quantities to forward with my own.

James Walter Lawry with his wife Charlotte, 1920s (Olive Lawry)

"From that day in the year 1863 when the first Cornish strawberries were sold in Covent Garden, the Tamar Valley fruit industry became a fact, and has been the means of enriching the neighbourhood, and supplying the needs of distant populations."

Having stumbled upon "prices … hitherto undreamt of" by sending his strawberries to London where they fetched 2/6 (£5.23 in today's prices) a punnet, he quadrupled his acreage. Within a short time between forty and fifty pickers were gathering up to 3,000 punnets (a ton of strawberries) a day. To keep fruit cool picking began at 4am. The first strawberries were usually ready by about 23 May.

Strawberry growing rapidly expanded into the neighbouring parishes as well as throughout St Dominick. Every available piece of sheltered south-facing land was seized and planted with strawberries. Oak woods were "ripped", (often with dynamite), their fertile slopes producing immense crops of strawberries. Special tools were made to work these slopes, the sclum and dibber. "Many working men in 1863, by acquiring patches of land, often woodland or furze (heath)… brought immediate and lucrative return." - *Lawry*. St Dominick alone was sending away over 250 tons of strawberries a season by the 1890s.

Lawry, a man of immense energy and enterprise, also established a further industry, punnet making. Following great difficulties in procuring these and after some experimentation, round half-pound punnets were made as a local cottage industry during the winter months. They were made from planed interlaced wood and sold by the gross. Someone skilled could make three gross a day earning ten pence a gross. Boxes holding fifty-four punnets were used. The filled punnets were placed in boxes and packed down with ferns to protect them in transit. For every ten pickers one cut ferns for packing. By the 1890s several local punnet factories had been established.

Lawry also negotiated with railway companies to secure the fastest routes, ensuring his fruit arrived early enough to fetch the best prices. As a result fruit gathered before 6am in Cornwall could be in the market in Edinburgh by 6am the following morning. Speed was vital.

The *Lord Grosvenor* apple introduced into the area by Lawry became known as *Lawry's No 1* or simply *No 1* and the local apple *Colloggett Pippin* was also called after him, *Lawry's Cornish Giant*. He was one of the first growers to introduce the Victoria plum to the valley where it was grown principally for jam.

In about 1900 Lawry and his wife Charlotte left Bohetherick Farm and moved to Tharsis in Calstock. Bohetherick Farm was split between nine tenants. Lawry embarked on a second career as a wool and agricultural merchant in Kelly Bray. He was a strong Methodist and a lay preacher. Following the death of his son in the First World War he became an advocate of the League of Nations, addressing meetings to gain support. He died on 15 August 1931 aged ninety-one.

Marketing the produce

Covent Garden Market, established in 1670 by the 4th Earl of Bedford (who had extensive estates in the Tamar Valley) became London's main fruit and vegetable market. It was to this market that Lawry's first fruit went. John Osborne of Covent Garden took a large proportion of the strawberries from the Tamar Valley. Lawry also sent fruit to Edinburgh and other provincial markets. Once significant quantities of flowers were grown, these too were sent to the London markets and many growers later found that they achieved better prices for their fruit in the provincial markets.

However "if there was too much stuff the commissioned salesmen would cut against each other in a day taking ridiculously low prices and then it would take several days for the price to come up again. We sent to J C Lucas, Sheffield, who wouldn't sell dirt cheap." - *Alan Langsford*. "Most of our flowers went to London J & E Page and George Monro, Covent Garden." - *Douglas Richards*. New Covent Garden Flower wholesaler Terry Moss sold Tamar Valley flowers: "It was known for high quality produce. We sold *Double Whites* - we rarely see it now. *Fortune*, *King Alfred* - they've gone. Most flowers have their time."

Generations of Tamar Valley women took their produce down river to Devonport Market. There had been a market there since the 1760s. River traffic declined as road transport increased and by the 1930s more growers were taking their produce to Plymouth Market, which was more easily reached by road. Both markets were bombed in 1941 and although Devonport was little damaged it never recovered. However some growers "never went further than Devonport" not moving until it closed. The traders in Plymouth market had to move onto the streets to make room for damaged chain stores. This became known as Tin Pan Alley. In 1959 a new market in Plymouth was built at Frankfort Gate.

Transport by river

For centuries the River Tamar was the main artery of the valley. Almost every farm had its own quay and there were ancient ferry crossings and market boats sharing the water with barges and schooners carrying ore, stone and heavy goods to and from the mines. Pack horses, wagons and tramways brought the goods down to the river bank. Many farmers and gardeners developed the skills of the mariner with those of farming or horticulture, carrying their produce to market and returning with dock dung.

The increase in motor transport during the First World War led to the decline in horse transport which, along with the railway, had begun to eclipse the use of the river. Excursion boats continued to ply the river and the market boats continued until the 1930s, but any large goods began to be transported by road. The "Empress" (1880 - 1926), a paddle steamer, was one of the best known market boats calling at every main quay either side of the river, arriving at North Corner, Devonport, with its cargo of market sellers and their produce. Worth's of Calstock ran a smaller market boat called the "Princess" every Friday until the 1930s. The Richards of Cargreen also had a small market boat running from Cargreen to Devonport in the 1920s and 1930s.

Captain Kitt's barge, Tamerton Lake

Transport by rail

Brunel's Great Western Railway arrived in Plymouth in 1849 and reached Cornwall in 1859 with the building of Saltash Bridge over the Tamar. Once Lawry started sending strawberries away from Saltash and Plymouth by rail others quickly followed.

The growers in the Bere Peninsula traditionally reached Plymouth Station by boat and cart. However in 1890 the London and South Western Railway reached Bere Alston and Bere Ferrers, opening the up-country market to more growers. Within a matter of months the South Western had poached much of the Great Western's fruit traffic. Its agents took fruit across by boat from Cotehele Quay to be collected by wagons for Bere Alston station. At Thorn Point they collected the growers' produce from Cargreen taking it to Bere Ferrers station. In 1908 the Calstock Viaduct was built over the river, connecting Bere Alston to Calstock, Gunnislake, Chilsworthy and Latchley. This stimulated further growth in fruit production in the Stoke Climsland area.

The "Earl of Mount Edgcumbe" (John Snell)

Lone rail truck at Calstock Station, 1968 (John Snell)

In 1966 the notorious cuts imposed by Beeching's reorganisation of the national rail system had a severe impact and many of the local stations were left unmanned. This marked the beginning of the end of the industry. Increased freight charges quickly followed and soon freight services completely ceased. Local grower H W Sherrell described this calamity as "The death blow to the valley's horticultural industry as we have known it". Fred Rogers collected produce from station wagons at Calstock and took it to Saltash station until it too lost its staff in 1967. Produce was then taken into Plymouth station. The loss of rail transport had an enormous impact on the very rapid decline in market gardening just as its arrival in 1859 had shaped its rapid growth. Once fruit could no longer be delivered to the markets within twenty-four hours it ceased to be sent.

Many growers turned to selling by direct purchase ('Pick Your Own') as well as to the local markets.

Growers today rely on road transport, some sending to wholesale markets up-country like Barry Richards and Gerald Veale (as well as locally). The Rickards' alstroemeria is sent by road to a major supermarket's distribution centre. Other growers like the Cradicks, Martin Crowell, Nigel Hunn, the Schuttkackers, Joe Collins, the Braunds, and Roy Clarke sell their flowers and produce locally to shops, restaurants and wholesalers. The Lukes, the only remaining Pick Your Own business, also sell locally. The large nurseries export their plants internationally as well as selling them all over Britain.

St Dominick Parish, Cornwall

Halton Quay

Olive Lawry

"My grandfather started it all"

Olive Lawry is the granddaughter of James Walter Lawry. She and her sister May grew up on their father's farm, Lynher Farm, North Hill.

Olive's father, Walter, had not taken over Bohetherick Farm when his father gave it up in 1900. He preferred to settle to the gentler pace of farming "unlike my grandfather who was a driver." Bohetherick Farm was split up into nine parts. At North Hill, Isaac Foot's sons used to come and spend their summers with them.

When Olive's parents retired they went to live near Callington in the house in which she still lives. She has always grown flowers and vegetables and continues to sell anemones at the local Womens' Institute market. She remembers the Vosper sisters at Bohetherick bunching up reeds from the river and selling them as "Tamar Spirea".

Olive remembers many trips from Lynher Farm to St Dominick as a child to collect cherries: "We had two twelve-pound baskets and bottled them". They were made into cherry pies for high teas on Sundays. "A cherry pie was better than anything." Olive still bottles gooseberries and redcurrants from her garden.

The Farm Prize Clock presented to J W Lawry in 1890

George and Freda Brown

"When we started out if you could live you were doing reasonably well and if you had a few pennies at the end of the year you were doing well!"

George and his wife Freda market gardened together from their marriage in 1941 until their retirement in 1985. In the 1960s they took on a plot of steeply sloping - 1:3 - south-facing land in the busy Cleeve Valley at Boars Bridge. By the time they "packed up" there was only one other gardener left there.

In 1973 after a very dry summer when the Browns had finally finished planting anemones they had their worst disaster: "That evening we had a violent thunder storm, 150 tons of soil washed clean right out. The anemones and strawberries all washed down. We picked up corms by the bucketful. Heck of a job to get it all back round! A tractor and digger broke the back of it". The steep garden had to be prepared again and the anemones replanted. It was very costly and soul destroying.

They worked the garden mainly by hand using tools made by the St Dominick blacksmith, Hughes, "an excellent blacksmith who hand-forged hoes, dibbers and sclums for the work." They grew strawberries, some under cloches. A winch was used (now at Cotehele Quay) to plough up their steep slope and to draw up eroded soil in a large scoop. Freda had to manage the winch, a job she loathed : "I hated it".

"We were the earliest in the country. We used to supply Marks and Spencer's with strawberries before supermarkets came in. They would pay you a good price taking anything you had from the end of May to the beginning of June… stop you overnight when Lincolnshire came in - they could do what they liked, they'd squeeze, squeeze and squeeze."

17

Veale Family

"I've been gardening for sixty-four years."

Gerald started at the age of fourteen when he left St Mellion School to work for his father. Both Gerald Veale's sons Andrew and Peter are still in the business. Andrew and his wife work the adjoining land at Woodlands. Peter and his daughters Sarah and Claire work with his parents.

The Veales were the first growers in the district to start growing pittosporum for foliage in 1936, and most of the pittosporum in the area has originated from their plants. Gerald also introduced eucalyptus when he started buying seed from Australia. These seedlings took two to three years to establish before they could be cut. He found it quite profitable when he started. Since then acres of eucalyptus have been planted and the price is much lower. However many growers don't have the same exacting standards as the Veale family. They have always been perfectionists in the production and presentation of their foliage.

In the 1960s they joined 'Starpack' who paid equal prices to all growers. The Veales felt that they were subsidising poor growers and were glad to leave it. They have been happier trading separately, and since the closure of the railway at Saltash their produce is taken away by lorry twice a week to wholesale markets. They grow strawberries, raspberries and pinks in polytunnels.

Their land covers a swathe of what used to be part of Lawry's Bohetherick Farm and sweeps down to the Tamar. The landscape has changed very little apart from the loss of fruit trees, which once covered much of the hillside down to Cotehele Quay. It was once known as Cherry Gardens.

Peter and Gerald Veale

Andrew Veale

Sarah and Claire

19

Natalie Allen

"I still think of Birchenhayes as being home."

Natalie Allen grew up on this sixty-eight acre farm which formed part of the Pentillie Estate. The land had been worked by her great-grandfather, William Parken, since 1871 and eight years later a local miller, James Dymond Langsford, married William's daughter Jane and moved to Birchenhayes. Their eldest son Reginald was Natalie's father and he took over the farm on his father's death in 1924.

James and his father-in-law ripped six acres of south-facing scrubland known as Brentswood and planted cherry gribbles which they grafted with black cherries. It is not known where they obtained the first grafts, but they named one variety *Birchenhayes Early*. Other types were *Upright, the Burcombe* (named after the Parken's neighbouring farm) and *Fice.* "You could never find a cherry that's as good as the Tamar Valley cherry." These trees were to form part of the famous Tamar Valley cherry orchards and provided a living for the family until the mid-1950s. Her mother, Laura Martin, was a proficient cherry picker and would climb the forty bar ladders only needing occasional help to shift the ladders from "coose to coose".

Laura's parents also worked a few acres at Brentswood and as a young woman Laura would be picking strawberries by 5.30am in heavy dew, wearing long skirts and warned by her mother "on no account let anyone see your ankles!" Grandma Martin spent all day on the land and cooked on a brandis over an open fire in their packing house.

Reginald Langsford also grew over fifty varieties of daffodils and by the age of seven Natalie and her older sister and three evacuee children were capable pickers and could recall the names of each variety. Daffodils were marketed in full bloom and her father took great pride in their presentation "ruffling the blossoms in their boxes". Natalie remembers her childhood at Birchenhayes with great fondness and will never forget the freedom and simple joys of playing on the farm with her constant companion, a large cockerel, tucked under one arm.

Terry and Vivian Rogers

"When I think back to the time when we were boys, my earliest memory is the sterilising plant."

As boys Terry and Vivian "loved to stoke the boiler". This was for the Hot Water Treatment Plant commercially pioneered by their father Fred Rogers in the 1920s to destroy eelworm, which bored into the centre of bulbs killing them. It was a major threat to the valley's industry. Their father Fred Rogers became well known throughout the South West as a leading horticulturist serving on many committees and doing an enormous amount for the Tamar Valley horticultural industry.

After the war they installed a state of the art, oil-fired boiler, which Vivian ran and helped to develop. At first they used mercury, handling it with ordinary gloves. A Ministry advisor on seeing this said they were lucky to be alive. They switched to formalin, which was less lethal.

The Rogers sold Gramoxone "which we used like water in those days" and DDT for dusting gooseberry bushes, "crazy but we didn't know".

They also sold fertilizer; formerly the growers had used dock dung. "Even today you can still see broken pieces of china, marbles, we used to pick up plenty of marbles."

Vivian remembers when daffodils had "all to be out" and bunches of twelve were tied with raffia about twenty-four fitting into a box. They'd be taken off to the train and telegrams would arrive from the wholesaler saying how much they'd made. Their daffodil flowers were later than Penzance, but earlier than Lincolnshire and as long as they "occupied this space then they were okay." There was a surplus of fruit before the Second World War and Fred Rogers decided to build a canning plant. However, war broke out and prices rocketed: "You could sell all the fruit".

As growers moved off the hills onto the flatter areas the Rogers' contracting business expanded. This meant that instead of planting daffodils by hand they could plant a furrow - placing the bulbs the right way up. "A big development" came when growers realised the bulbs didn't have to be upright and they banked them up like potatoes. "That was the beginning of the end really, the slopes couldn't compete."

Vivian and Terry

Joyce and Alan Rickard

"I was born and bred into it."

Alan and his wife Joyce have known one another since childhood. Both their families were market gardeners. Joyce remembers picking primroses, which sometimes made more money than the daffodils.

Alan's father Westlake Rickard returned home after a period as a miner in Canada to take on five acres of Brentswood. He grew cherries, dahlias, rhubarb, irises, strawberries and daffodils. *"Mags [Magnificence] -* they weren't a good flowerer, but was early, usually the first out by February 23rd ". The daffodils stayed in the ground for three years followed by potatoes for a year and then a three-year crop of strawberries. The work was all done by hand. All the gardeners at Brentswood had "earth cars" to draw up the soil which had fallen to the bottom of the steep slopes.

They sold their produce "mainly local in Plymouth". To beat growers on the Saltash Ferry the Rickards would drive across the moor via Tavistock to Plymouth, getting up at 4am. In 1948 they joined the exodus from the slopes to flatter land where mechanisation was possible.

Then in 1957 Alan and Joyce started building their first glasshouse. Their son Brian joined them and they have become one of the biggest producers of alstroemeria (Peruvian Lily) in the country on their five acres of glass. Their glasshouses are computerised, and have bunching machines that get through 2,000 bunches an hour. They have a workforce of sixteen. Alstroemeria are grown under licence, which controls the price. They are grown on a three-year rotation when new tubers are planted. Despite growing one crop for thirty years Alan finds alstroemeria growing fascinating "every year is different".

Courtney Vanstone

"There were orchards everywhere."

Courtney Vanstone began working for Mr Herring at Bohetherick Farm after leaving school. He picked cherries and liked the *Burcombes* best. Three or four "windtackers" were put in the orchards to scare the birds and sheets of "galvanised" were beaten. His grandfather was George Striplin who made cherry ladders and punnets.

He took on two and a half acres of steep land at Cotehele Quay, "barren" but for one solitary *American Mother*, "a beautiful apple". It took eighteen months to clear the ground by hand and get it into production. Here he grew daffodils, (*Brilliancy* and *Helios*), irises, anemones, lettuce, pittosporum and spring cabbage. He always suffered with daffodil rash. It would creep up his arms making them "raw terrible" and even get into his eyes. When he stopped picking it would disappear. He worked in the woods for the National Trust and also helped the salmon fisherman Charles Nilsson (Nelson), "one of the best".

In 1953 he married Margaret, a former evacuee who had lived at Birchenhayes Farm during the War. When their daughter was born they'd take her down to the gardens for the day's work, and as a toddler she'd "bunch leaves" alongside her mother. They took on four and a half acres of flat land at Pitt Meadow. There they grew leeks and gooseberries (*Leveller* and *Careless*) and one year they picked two tons. Their early strawberries "went up the line", but as the season went on they were sold locally. During the summer they'd be up at 5am working on the garden.

Like most of the market gardeners Courtney always carried a gun up to his garden to shoot the rabbits. He had three ferrets and would go rabbiting during the winter. He still loves walking through Cotehele Woods: "I know almost every tree in the wood, every rabbit hole and foxhole".

Nigel and Wendy Hunn

"We still grow a lot of strawberries!"

Nigel and Wendy Hunn's families have been market gardening in St Dominick for generations. Nigel still "rents a field down the road that grandfather (Lewis Trenance) took in 1900". His father had six or seven acres of strawberries, daffodils and spring cabbage. Nigel and his sons work seventy acres including "the best part of two acres glass and two acres tunnels". They are among the few remaining families still in horticulture full-time.

Nigel remembers his father growing "*King Alfred*, *Sunrise*, back then *Cambridge 134*, (strawberries) when I left school and *Cambridge Vigour*, a very dark strawberry, used to fill the punnets". *Elsanta* is the variety that they grow most of today "nice flavour, good cropper". His father used to pay a workman £5 a week to hand hoe for most of the summer. They bought all their boxes, cloches and supplies from Fred Rogers: "they used to give a good service actually".

Nigel's father was a good shot and would spend several days a week during the winter shooting on neighbouring farms. Nigel also liked shooting. "I was a very good shot". He remembers waiting for daylight at 4.30-5am so that they could cut cabbage. A crate of cabbages doesn't make any more money now than it did twenty years ago: "a crate of cabbage was £1, now its £2 - £2.50".

Nigel Hunn

Darren, Wendy and Ian

Liam Hunn

Roy Clarke

"We prick out every single plant ourselves."

Roy Clarke and his wife Joan work together on five acres growing bedding plants, daffodils and pinks. Roy grows strawberries "for my friends."

He used to grow *Gorella*, "the best strawberry I ever had, that was handsome". He picks pinks twice a week over a long season, from May to autumn : "they flower, then they start again another crop come autumn time". He has help bunching the pinks, apart from which he and his wife do everything themselves. He used to grow anemones but they became disease prone. The last time he grew them he planted 20,000 and "none came up whatsoever". This year he's growing them in a polytunnel and hoping for better results. Years ago, "everybody would plant a 5,000 pack of anemone corms for themselves, so they could sell a little. My father planted *Double Whites* all the way round the house and made a half a crown a bunch fifty years ago". Roy sells his flowers and plants to local Spar shops. He used to pick cherries at Bohetherick Farm. "The last time (five years ago) there was cherries down there five people were picking them and four of them were over eighty!"

He spent years fishing salmon with Ivan Cradick. "When I first used to catch fish, in April, they'd be jumping all the way round the boat. We always did two tides, half an hour each side of high or low water." There used to be cuckoos flying across the river when he was out fishing. They took the catch to Stan Langsford at Cotehele Quay, whatever the time of night; they would knock calling, "Stan, fish!"

Roy still uses many of his old tools, especially the dibber. "How would you plant without a dibber? I've used that every other day." Roy also uses the old Colewood single wheeled motor hoe, which gets into any awkward corner. He spends his winters shooting - it used to be rabbits, now its pheasants : "It's all I live for".

Joe Collins

"I've been in this job since I could walk, ever since mother could get me in a pushchair to take me to the garden! 'Tis in your blood something grow'd up with you."

Joe Collins' father and mother worked five acres of steep ground at Stockwell Farm, St Dominick. "Everything had to be carried from bottom to top."

His mother and another worker once dug a ton of potatoes in a day, "it was hard work back in they days". They had apples, *American Mother* "a beautiful apple to keep for Christmas", and cherry trees. In the 1940s their *Bullion* and *Burcombe* cherries fetched fifteen shillings for a a twelve-pound chip - "cherries was good money". He remembers the famous Plymouth Argyle goalkeeper Les Major running down through Brentswood barefoot, climbing cherry trees after a friendly game.

Their strawberries also fetched good prices then (two shillings a chip). His parents employed twenty to twenty-five pickers. Joe has twelve acres of gardens running down to Halton Quay. He has three acres of eucalyptus and the rest are polytunnels of strawberries, scabious, pinks, dahlias and anemones. Although Joe has always worked on the garden part-time his son Adrian is full-time. Joe's wife Gwen does all the bunching. Eucalyptus gives them a "steady winter keep" and the spring and summer crops bring in the "bread and butter."

Joe is proudest of his strawberry crop. This year he has tried a new variety called *Elsa:* "absolutely fantastic. They smell absolutely out of this world. They taste like a real strawberry". They're sold from his house and to local shops. "I grow them the old fashioned way." He imports bumblebees from Holland to pollinate his fruit and flowers. He's always kept bees, "essential they are". They pollinate all the crops and are particularly important for the runner beans.

Because of this he gets well formed strawberries from the beginning of the season, the hard knotty centre becoming a perfectly shaped fruit. "Strawberries, that's my speciality, my father would be some proud if he could see me now." Joe does all the strawberry picking himself.

Raspberry pickers, including Gladys Johns, with Chris Heron at Woodlands Farm, St Mellion, 1920s (Brenda Johns)

Hoeing anemones at Ellbridge, c.1950 (Ellbridge)

Mary Martin and Virginia Spiers

"Brentswood was special."

Mary Martin and her sister Virginia Spiers grew up in St Dominick.

Mary Martin is a well-known landscape artist and has been painting the changing landscapes of the Tamar Valley over the last thirty years. Her sister Virginia writes a regular "Country Diary" for the "Guardian". Mary and her partner James Evans have spent years researching, collecting and grafting Tamar varieties of apples and cherries, which would otherwise have disappeared. These now form the nucleus of a five acre orchard that they have planted, a mother orchard containing a Tamar gene bank of local varieties. Their illustrated book about the valley's market gardens and orchards *"Burcombes, Queenies and Colloggetts"* was published in 1996.

Their parents farmed and they are related to many local families. In the season, as children, they occasionally helped pick fruit. "We'd eat ourselves crazy…strawberries so red, so luscious."

A grower's daughter told them that they bunched irises on the kitchen table and that "Just when we could see the table through the irises father would bring in another bucket to bunch!" They remember the anemones, "great fields of them".

Some people sent away nosegays of flowers, which made a lot of money. Mary and Virginia used to pick primroses. Each bunch was made with twelve flowers and three leaves. These were fastened with a rubber band. "We'd put boxes on the 76 bus at Ashton, give them to the bus conductor and he'd hand them over to the stationmaster at Saltash." In the depths of winter they once gathered moss for John Friendship who supplied florists.

At Brentswood they remember growers cultivating Devon violets, polyanthus and kaffir lilies - "just such a lot of energy to get a cash crop". People grew a lot of foliage too, eucalyptus, pittosporum, escallonia and white tree heather.

Mary and Virginia

Brian Johns

"When I was a boy I used to rotovate up under the trees before school."

Brian took over Dairy Mill Farm from his father Ron who had the tenancy from 1940. Ron's father Heber was a market gardener at Mount Pleasant (next door to George Brown's father).

Brian can remember the five and a half acres of orchards when they were planted up with bulbs - *Actaea, Emperor, Victoria* and *Double Whites*. He remembers a "piece" of polyanthus and anemones his father grew. Potatoes and plums grew in Plum Garden (*Rivers* and *Victoria*). There were also a few old cherries on Cherry Hill where his grandfather Heber fell out of a cherry tree in 1940. He had to wear a raised boot for the rest of his life.

Brian's mother Gwen would bring the daffodils into the house to force them into flower. "The smell of them was out of this world, it was handsome. Mother used to work a lot on the farm. She also did the bunching of the flowers." They sent the flowers away to R C Cole of Covent Garden, and some to Birmingham. There is still a field called Rhubarb Field although Brian can't remember ever seeing any growing.

The apple orchards used to have *Worcester, American Mother, Charles Ross, Coxes Orange, Lanes, Excelsior, Russet, Lord Derby* and *Gladstone* and *Conference* pears growing in them: "I like the old Gladstones."

Ron Johns had a couple of workmen on the farm; one was Stan Harris. During the war Italian POWs from the camp at Callington also helped. The Congdon family had seventeen acres of market garden at Dairy Mill Farm in the 1860s. Pickers would come and stay in the barn and packing sheds which both have chimneys.

Ron is still working on the farm although in 1983 he handed it on to his son and daughter-in-law Brenda, who subsequently bought it.

Brian and Ron

Norma Chapman

"We'd sing our hearts out up the trees it was lovely right out across the valley!"

Norma's parents, the Sambles, market gardened on the steep slopes of Brentswood where she worked alongside them.

Her father's birthday was 21 February and "if he'd pick flowers on his birthday it was an early season". They'd have sixty to eighty buckets full of daffodils at a time waiting to be bunched, and "we always saw the beauty of them."

When Norma's daughter was born she was taken to the plot. If it rained she would play in the ladder house where all the ladders were kept for cherry picking. They had forty-one rung ladders and the smallest were twenty bar. They had hundreds of cherry trees some of which her father had grafted. They'd collect three to four tons of fruit a year generally. In their best year they got eight tons and in their worst twenty pounds. "My mother used to absolutely adore picking cherries. You'd see all the cherries pitching in the tree."

It was a skilled job and could take all day to pick around the ladder. Cherry time was always very busy. There was "such demand for cherries, almost all sold before they came off the tree".

They had a well at Brentswood: "it was the cleanest and purest water".

Geoffrey and Sylvia Mason

"The blossom would look beautiful, beautiful…"

Geoffrey and Sylvia Mason gardened at Braunder, seven acres of steep sloping land between Dairy Mill Farm and Halton Quay. Geoffrey's grandmother Sarah Mason bought the holding in 1860 from the Frise family who'd built the house and ripped the hillside in 1836. An enormous wall was built and covered in trained fruit.

The Pentillie Estate owned the surrounding land, and the Masons paid a token of a shilling to pick ferns from Viverdon Down to line strawberry punnets. They had "*Queens*, red right through", *Worcester Pearmain*, red and green *Bramley, Lane's Prince Albert, Jubilee* (cooker) and *American Mother*: "a lot of they." They also had *Czars* and *Early Rivers* plums (one year they picked 700 twelve pound chips). Geoffrey and his father sold their produce at Plymouth market three times a week, selling it off the back of their van.

His father kept bees in hives and butts (skeps). Geoffrey remembers picking cherries in Julys so cold that he was wearing an overcoat up the thirty to forty bar ladders: "could hardly stand up it was blowing a gale. Us all had cherries. Looked up the valley it was handsome".

In 1947 Geoffrey married Sylvia. She was the granddaughter of Richard Striplin, a carpenter who made punnets, cherry ladders and the packing sheds of Brentwood. Sylvia's father and uncle "were in a couple of carpentry shops in copper mines in Phoenix, Arizona". Her father fought in the American army in the First World War.

Geoffrey had always wanted to become a mechanic, but he had to work on the holding after leaving school. In 1971, Geoffrey's brother and sister retired and Braunder was sold. He went to work for Alan Rickard at Lanoyce: "loved it, worked from October 1971 until 1992".

43

Pop Courtis

"I've been fishing since I was eleven year old and I still do it. It's got very poor now. We only get one or two salmon. One time you could pack up a job and go salmon fishing."

Pop left school at twelve and went to work on Edward Rickard's ground in Comfort Wood, Cotehele.

They had three acres, "a lot of *Sovereigns* and *Febes* and *Huxley Giant. Sovereign* were much sweeter. When the fruit was on you could smell it down the valley". Buyers would collect the produce from the plot. "I got fifteen shillings a week but one pound when the fruit season was on. One chap called Harper would take hundreds of two pound chips in a lorry". Before the war they didn't use any chemicals and "castor meal and cocoa shells was a nice slow feeder for strawberries."

While working in Luckett mine he got the name "Pop." When the chute he was working in got blocked he'd climb up with a stick of dynamite to give it a "pop" to clear it. He also had thirteen months at Kit Hill mine. "I went to Kit Hill, we did a project there for Aldermaston for shock waves underground. I cut the chambers out. The Americans said you couldn't cut a six foot round ball of solid granite but we did it."

He always kept a bit of ground. "I used to do it for a bit of peace and quiet after a day on the roads, get away from the jack hammer." For years he's had bees: "You've got to have they for pollination." In the winter he's a beater on shoots when there is little to do in the garden "down to the flat hours."

He used to pick cherries at Morden Farm for the Langsford family. "One year picked six ton all in twelve pound chips." Marquands (a local wholesaler) would come and collect them. The cherries were so plentiful that he picked two dozen pounds an hour that year. "You always had one leg through the bar then you could pick with both hands. You'd tie a rope through a limb of the tree to stop the ladder running away with you."

He still has a garden near Cotehele and grey squirrels are his biggest problem: "them sinners!" His strawberry crop was ruined one year. "The devils had them all picked in heaps!"

Albert Wills

"In 1925 my brother Sydney ploughed the field (Ellbridge Experimental Station) for them with a pony and plough."

Albert, the son of Bessie and Ben Wills, grew up at Ellbridge on a five acre market garden.

He went to Landulph School and remembers the Cherry Feast at Pentillie. When Landulph School lost its church school status the children were no longer invited to Pentillie, and so two local families, the Richards and the Nanscowans, "got up their own cherry feast".

They grew strawberries, raspberries, rhubarb, blackcurrants, gooseberries, plums, apples and vegetables. Albert remembers Plymouth Co-op collecting tubs of raspberries and blackcurrants for their jam factory. All the way along the road from Saltash to St Dominick wooden jam tubs stood by the roadside waiting for the lorry.

At Strawberry Hill they would take the tubs to the Co-op's lorry at Halton Quay. Albert and his father took their produce to the Co-op's depot at the Barbican in Plymouth. The Co-op then distributed the goods to their shops using ten wagons and horses.

Rita (Albert's daughter) took several van loads of produce to Saltash station each day. "It was always frantic getting to the station, always last minute!" They grew two to three acres of strawberries, *Huxley's Giant*, *Feebs* and *Favourite* and had 3,000 cloches. Their strawberries had few diseases, as they were able to rotate the crops easily on their large acreage. They sold to Woolworth's in Plymouth, who would send a van out to Strawberry Hill for more punnets if they had sold out.

In 1972 Albert retired after forty years at Strawberry Hill and it became farmland. The orchards and hedges were taken out, and everything was ploughed up.

(Chris Chapman)

Alwyn Green's King Alfreds, 1950s (Alan Preston)

Calstock Parish, Cornwall

Picking Cheerfulness bulbs, 1953, Brian and Mim Stephens and Elsie Studden

John Lanyon

"Firetail, Lucifer and Seagull."

When John Lanyon became Head Gardener at Cotehele House five years ago he was intrigued by the lines of daffodils that studded the estate. He soon discovered that these were a legacy of the market gardening industry.

Helped by local experts he began to identify the flowers. A leading daffodil grower in the valley, Dan du Plessis, gave him encouragement, advice and bulbs that he'd bred whilst others gave him old varieties like *"Butter and Eggs."* John now has a collection of over 400 varieties, many of them old-fashioned.

These have been planted in the orchard at Cotehele which contains a collection of Tamar Valley fruit trees. His favourite daffodil is *Firetail,* which is a very delicate star-like flower. John has a full-time staff of three who are developing the fourteen and a half acre gardens and also maintaining their collection of daffodils. These represent many of the varieties formerly grown on the Cotehele Estate. John now holds a Daffodil Show every spring at Cotehele, when hundreds of old varieties are displayed in the house.

(Chris Chapman)

Martin Crowell

"Back in the winter I had a robin I could feed in my hand."

Martin is still market gardening the same twelve and a half acres as his father. He grows sweet peas, pinks, Sweet William, strawberries, daffodils, runner beans, cabbage, chrysanthemums, parsley and rhubarb.

Originally the garden was larger but Cotehele built a car park on their *Double White* field many years ago. "All *Double Whites* in the car park, half a crown a bunch back then." Martin used to send them to William Hardy of Newcastle. "Used to be ringing for them. Before Beeching cut the line you could send them away on the twenty past ten and they'd be in Newcastle the next day." He is one of the few growers left selling them.

Martin's grandfather, William Martin, had a packing shed at Bohetherick with an old tortoise stove. It was kept going all night to force flowers. Growers put shelves around them to hold the flower buckets. As a child Martin slept in a little bunk there.

Martin's wife May grew up in Calstock, the daughter of one of the largest tomato growers there. "Calstock used to produce 100 tons of tomatoes a week. I remember going on the market boat to Devonport." May used to gorge on split Tamar cherries that a school friend brought to school. The girl's uncle was blinded in the mines when he was eighteen and his family bought him a holding at Chilsworthy, where he grew cherries. Martin remembers Pop Courtis picking cherries at Morden farm, "like a monkey up sixty to seventy foot trees. There were cherries on the verges, all gone at Halton Quay… could go down and have your fill".

Martin always took a prize at St Dominick Flower Show for his anemones. Other growers would be up half the night getting their boxes of daffodils just so. Dutch bulb salesmen would come to the show to meet the growers. "It used to be there was a job for everyone in the valley."

Tony and Martin

53

Vivian Nelson

"When I left school there were twelve fishing boats just at Cotehele, four men to a boat, sixty men."

Vivian Nelson is one of a tiny group of specialists who fished the Tamar and in between tides worked a market garden. His grandfather was Charles Nilsson, a Scandinavian seaman who settled in Calstock. Vivian's father William was born in 1903 and along with his brother Charles worked on boats with their father.

They also collected "point stuff" which was used as fertiliser from the river. From 1948 the Nelson (originally Nilsson) family, including both brothers, lived at Cotehele Quay. The salmon fishing season used to be from March 2 to the end of August. In the 1950s and 1960s each of the salmon boats would catch sixty to seventy salmon in the best months of May and June: "biggest one I ever caught was twenty-eight pounds".

In 1960 he took over from Stan Langsford buying fish from other fishermen and in his best season he sold four tons of salmon. These went by train to Billingsgate via Calstock. When the service stopped he had to take salmon to the fish merchants of Plymouth and Saltash.

Before refrigeration the fish were wrapped in sycamore leaves covered in ferns and paper and packed in wooden crates.

In 1955, the family gave up their garden at Cotehele House, which is still known as "Nelsons Piece." Afterwards Jean and Vivian Nelson had a field of six acres that they gardened. Anemones gave them a winter income, planted in June and picked from September throughout the winter. They remember one year when the blooms of the daffodil *Fortune* were so big and opened-up that they could only fit nine bunches in a box, which normally held eighteen to two dozen. In May they picked *Double Whites* and irises, "dark blue *Imperator*, pale blue *Van Vleit* and yellow *Golden Harvest*".

The combination of market gardening and salmon fishing was exhausting. Vivian retired in 1994.

Mrs Jope

"If you weren't a Methodist in those days you didn't stand a chance. They had their fingers in every pie!"

Mrs Jope moved to Gunnislake when she was five and a half years old in 1919. It was a time of great change for the area as the mines had just closed and Bealswood Brickworks next to her home lay in ruins. There was little work available other than market gardening. Many of the miners had emigrated or were leaving and there was a shipping agent who sold tickets in the village.

She became a teacher at Calstock School and saw how market gardening influenced the lives of the children: "they were very commercially minded". They would pick pussy willow and primroses from the hedgerows sending them away with their parents' flowers.

The Paper Mill at Ivybridge sent out boxes of primroses to all its customers and so the children of Gunnislake picked for the Mill, as did many people around Ivybridge. Primroses were in great demand for Mothering Sunday and Easter Day. Children from the age of eight or nine would go picking. In the 1950s they'd get about 3d a bunch for them. In the strawberry season the children would fall asleep at their desks because as soon as the sun rose they would be out picking. Then after school they'd have to go picking again until sunset.

"I can remember Mr Lawry. He was a very dignified man, a very strong Methodist and a businessman, he moved from St Dominick to Tharsis, a house in Calstock."

(Chris Chapman)

57

Douglas Davy

"If they ever wonder why horticulture died, it died because the young people weren't prepared to accept it."

Douglas Davy's father came from Launceston to Calstock in the 1920s and set up a glasshouse business.

He specialised in tomatoes like most of the growers. Glasshouses were mainly concentrated in Calstock although there were also some in Cargreen. These tomatoes were particularly flavoursome because of the high potassium content of the soil and were very popular.

Douglas and his brother Kenneth followed their father into the industry. During the war Douglas joined the RAF and became a pilot. In 1945 he returned and set up a new nursery at Rosehill, which took several years to come into full production. His brother remained on the original site and between them they had half an acre of glass. The yearly crop rotation was tulips for the Christmas market followed by irises and then tomatoes.

Towards the end of his career Douglas grew show pinks, which had become fashionable. Douglas and his wife worked with two other workers.

In Calstock, which was dominated by market gardening, a large number of the working population had work for only nine months of the year, from March to October. When land work was slack they had to go on the dole. As Douglas says, "In all, if you look back on it, a very grim sort of life basically. The time between the wars was pretty poor. The war really improved the lot of the growers who for the first time felt that their industry had a future".

Ruth Wilcocks

"It was a sight, a sea of yellow beautifully kept."

Ruth Wilcocks was born by the Tamar at Netstakes, Gunnislake.

Along with other local children she learned to swim: "pay a penny to Mr Teague and would swim on the Gunnislake Weir". He was the ferryman taking people from the island to the Devon side in the 1930s and 1940s. Ruth worked for her mother-in-law picking and bunching on her five acres at Honicombe. At busy times she also worked for other growers such as Mr George Cradick of Calstock who had acres of spring flowers and iris. The men would pick and bring the flowers to the packing houses for the women to bunch and pack in green tissue paper to show off yellow flowers and blue tissue paper for white flowers. "They were all picked open and placed in the box, in two rows of twelve, flowers facing up" secured with thin wooden stakes. In 1953 Percy Thrower, the television gardener, filmed her and other bunchers at George Cradick's packing shed.

Ruth remembers the period after the war when every south-facing slope and field was cultivated: "From Gunnislake New Bridge to Harewood, Calstock, St Dominick and inland to St Ann's Chapel, Harrowbarrow, Honicombe, Danescombe. The fields looked beautiful everywhere in full bloom and rows of pickers working, it was all meticulously clean. Almost as if everyone was in competition." Even plots either side of the railway during the war had rhubarb in strips six foot wide: "Every little plot was cultivated!"

"You can't compare the strawberries we grew with those now for flavour." Ruth also worked at Calstock Chip Factory making chip baskets. "I was on the two pounds, I was excellent at it", but given any other size she was hopeless.

Alfie Striplin and others salmon fishing at Cotehele Quay, 1950s (Alec Friendship)

Pauls, Harewood - packing punnets with ferns (Brian Stephens)

Brian and Mim Stephens

"There were so many men needing work in Calstock that you always saw men picking flowers and fruit."

Brian Stephens and his brother Harold grew up at Lower Kelly, Calstock, next door to the Goss family (the boat builders).

Brian's parents market gardened at Higher Kelly. Mr Green had Kelly Gardens which was close to them and "so early and such wonderful ground it was priceless."

In 1944 the family moved up to the flatter land at Paramount, "a fair nursery". It had belonged to a Dutchman who'd gone off to fight in the war. Brian's father Fred specialised in anemones, planting 100,000 - 150,000 corms a year. He grew a lot of *King Alfred* daffodils. When he packed them "My father was very fussy, he'd make sure the full trumpet was always showing, looking perfect. He was very particular." They grew *Double Whites*, but it was the Friendship family at Harewood who had one of "the best strains". The Stephens also had an acre of *Royal Sovereign* strawberries, "they were the best". They had a "larger acreage" of *Febes*.

In the glasshouses they grew tomatoes including *Potenta* and *Stoners Exhibition* as well as cucumbers and lettuce. Tomato seedlings were bought from Fred Carter in Calstock and lettuce seedlings from the Braunds of Cargreen. Tomato seedlings were planted in March and they would start to pick in May.

In 1953 Brian married Mim Studden of Calstock. They put up 15,000 square feet of glass and grew lettuce, tomatoes, irises, freesias and Doris pinks. Mim got anemone rash and couldn't harvest them. The lettuce was grown through the winter "cutting for Christmas - best money". They generally picked 150 twelve pound chips of tomatoes a week and sold most of these to Tom Moore. He had the Salad Bowl in Plymouth Market specialising in high quality produce. "He buys locally to ensure maximum freshness and for the same reason makes daily collections from nurseries so that the salad materials on his stall have been cut only an hour or so earlier." (*17 December 1971, Western Daily Herald*).

In 1983 the combination of oil price increases (they used eight and a half gallons an hour) and the increasing competition forced them to sell up.

Dulcie Stephens

"Anemones were our prime thing."

Dulcie Stephens grew up at Stockadon Farm on the Pentillie Estate in Landulph, which her parents and grandparents farmed. She was born and spent many happy holidays at Berry Farm, St Dominick, with her maternal grandparents, who grew fruit and flowers.

In 1952 Dulcie married Harold Stephens, a third generation market gardener on land rented from the Bowhay Estate in Calstock. Harold worked a four and a half acre field growing strawberries and daffodils including *King Alfred, Fortune* and *Actaea*. He and Dulcie worked together and extended the strawberry season by growing some under cloches. In the strawberry season they would start picking at daybreak, employing extra help at times.

Harold used to say "you could tell a good strawberry picker by their hands". No stains meant a good picker. Dulcie always thought that the *Cambridge 422* strawberry had the best flavour.

Harold's favourite crop was anemones. Dulcie found picking them unbearable as they grew up to 80,000 corms a year. In the early days they shared machinery with Harold's father and brother, "a little Ransome tractor, then a Ferguson T20, a rotary hoe and a couple of one wheeled 2 stroke Colwood hoes". They took on more land after Harold's father died, getting a Massey Ferguson 135 and adding potatoes to their range of crops.

King Family

"We send the pinks by lorry to London, Manchester and Birmingham. Some go locally, like our ranunculus."

The Kings bought the ground in Harewood in 1959. At that time two elderly men, Bratchley and Cox, who kept their land "immaculately", worked the neighbouring ground. They took the produce to Calstock in a horse and cart.

The Kings have eight acres and Mrs King's son David now grows pinks, which go away by road twice a week along with those of other growers, such as the Veales of Bohetherick. Mrs King's husband worked in engineering but as he found less work he used the eight acres to supplement his income.

During the 1950s and 1960s Harewood was still full of gardens. Jean Symonds, a neighbour, grew narcissi, lily of the valley, muscari, strawberries and daffodils.

The Kings still have daffodils, which come up each year on the slopes that run down to the Tamar, but they no longer find it worthwhile to pick them. "Oh, the *Double Whites* used to smell beautiful, picked open the perfume was overpowering."

Sylvia, Yvette and David

69

Alec Scoble

"I've spent a life-time fishing on the Tamar."

Alec Scoble grew up at Waterside in Saltash. He started to fish as a schoolboy and "when I left school I went fishing for a living."

He married Gloria Wilton from Calstock whose mother Vera bought balls of cotton from Cloads of the Barbican (in Plymouth), and "made salmon nets through the winter." Alec would fill an old bath with tar, soaking his nets in it to preserve them: "the tar on new nets would burn your face". In Saltash the rope for net making was straightened by stretching it out dozens of times around the lamp-posts along the water-side. In Calstock it was stretched around the fields and roads.

"I couldn't afford to go fishing when I married", so Alec worked at Hingston Down Quarry, going fishing when he could. "My wife would grow a few anemones." Many of the fishermen "went picking flowers or fruit in between the tides". Alec remembers one particular fisherman who would sleep by the river between tides. "I've seen he morning's frost covered in, where he slept in a hedge to catch the tide early in the mornings, hard as nails, hard as nails."

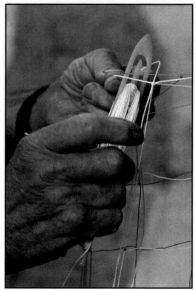

Mike Venning

"...thirty-four people working in this valley (Danescombe) when I was here, scattered around."

His father Fred and mother Alberta lived at Kellywood Cottage in the Danescombe Valley from 1955 - 1967, where they had three and a half acres. They "couldn't get into St Dominick" as it was impossible to get any land there.

When he was fourteen Fred Venning started working at Greenhill Arsenic Works lining arsenic barrels with paper. He also used to deliver dynamite and fuses to a mine in Latchley. He collected the explosives and carried them on his back through Gunnislake Clitters, Bitthams and on to the field below Latchley Hill.

There were acres of cherries growing there at that time and Fred remembered *Best Black* and *Morellos*. Men from the arsenic works got good money picking them after work and "there was more money for those who could climb high."

Mike grew strawberries, early potatoes and daffodils. He had irises and anemones. He also worked as a lorry driver as he couldn't make a living solely from market gardening.

The Danescombe Valley was two weeks earlier on the south side than on the flatter land higher up, and strawberries had long been the main crop there along with potatoes and daffodils. In the 1950s Mike can remember a local variety, called *"Tommy Friendship"*, being grown with the main strawberry of the period (*Madame Lefebvre*). Tommy Friendship had found it growing in Calstock churchyard and propagated it, according to his nephew the late John Friendship. It was very early with small, sweet purple-red berries. Another strawberry, *Rearguard*, used to turn blue before red, and had to be picked when they were half white and blushing red to ensure they were perfect by the time they'd reach market.

Top picture - Dorothy Start and her mother, Marguerite Preston, (on the right), with other Flemish refugees from the First World War, c.1923 (Dorothy Start)
Below - The Preston family and pickers, Kelly Gardens, Danescombe Valley, c.1909 (Alan Preston)

Charles and Bill Nelson salmon fishing opposite Symonds gardens at Cotehele c.1949 (Vivian Nelson)

Norman Trewartha

"Back in strawberry time, especially if you had a hot season, when I was a boy, you could smell the strawberries as you'd go by the patches."

Norman Trewartha and his uncle before him market gardened what had been a kitchen garden belonging to the Edgcumbe Estate at Cotehele.

The enormous garden wall still dominates the hillside overlooking the Danescombe Valley. Norman's uncle, Claude Fletcher, took over from the last kitchen gardener Ned Maunder. It was full of asparagus and artichoke beds and the walls covered in trained fruit - peaches, plums and pears. It also had cherry trees, mostly *Fice,* which Norman would pick for his uncle, who was unable to climb the ladders.

Norman and his wife Elsie married in 1956. They took over the garden and also worked two and a half acres at Butts, Calstock. In his early years "there was always a job in market gardening. People could start up and get a living from it. When we were boys we used to look across the valley to see who had the most weed. It was like a competition." Horace Loze grew the local *Tommy Friendship* strawberries: "He had 3,000 (plants) sent up-country".

As the prices dropped after the beginning of the season, traders would come and buy from the growers. "Granny Wakeham would come and pick up strawberries, she came from Bodmin. Hopper had a lorry and would come up from down Cornwall."

After so many years working the gardens there Norman can't bear to see it as it is now: "I'm ashamed to go there now". Traces of market gardening can still be seen in the lines of pittosporum and collapsing packing sheds. The daffodils still flower in their lines each spring.

Alan Elias

"I can remember Mike Pollock arriving at Ellbridge."

Alan Elias married Ann, the daughter of the grower George Lane of Rising Sun, Harrowbarrow.

While working for his father-in-law he started gradually to "put up Dutch lights" on a field nearby. He left to drive an egg-collecting lorry for Devon and Cornwall Eggs.

"The last time I grew early potatoes all the girls (eight) came down from the packing station (Devon and Cornwall Eggs at Callington) to help! I took a ton of potatoes in early May and they made £19 - I was lucky to get that - a French boat had docked in Plymouth full of potatoes!"

He used to grow *Ailsa Craig, Moneymaker* and *Primset* tomatoes. At one time he harvested a ton of runner beans a week getting tuppence for a pound. He remembers Mr Stone, a grower from Ferry Farm, Calstock who specialised in early runner beans refusing to sell them for less than sixpence a pound. "He came in early and had a complete set up. He had one man who did nothing else but water the beans!" Alan sent his pinks to T J Poupart at Bristol and tomatoes to Exeter via Gunnislake station. He never joined 'Starpack', as he couldn't see the point in paying "two loads of commission."

He runs Rising Sun Nurseries with his family and a few part-time workers. He still grows pinks and bedding plants, selling in Tavistock and Holsworthy markets as he has done for thirty years. In 1991 he built a new Garden Centre and café at Rising Sun, Harrowbarrow, which has continued to grow and flourish.

John Trebilcock

"I used to know every flower."

John Trebilcock was one of ten children and grew up in St Ann's Chapel. By the age of fourteen he was working in the Silver Valley wolfram mine. When he was sixteen he started market gardening for Blight Brothers of Harrowbarrow, where he stayed until they closed. For the last twenty years he has worked at Rising Sun Nurseries.

Blight Brothers was "the biggest concern in Harrowbarrow". They had acres of strawberries and picked 1,000 two-pound chips a day in the period before the war. "They made £1,000 a day!" They grew "*Feebs* - 'twas a good strawberry - and *Huxley Giant* was a later one." They were sold in Plymouth. They also had fourteen acres of daffodils that Jack and the men picked. The women used to do the bunching at Blight Bros. They were sent away by rail: "I've seen Gunnislake station piled high".

The business had a fleet of seven lorries delivering and collecting produce from various growers. They went up to Evesham to collect plums and apples in the 1960s. The Blights had their own Bramley orchards and used to take vegetables to Dartmoor Prison: "the kale went to Plymouth and spring cabbage to them. They were having the best out there!"

In the evenings he'd go fishing, working the tides: "we'd do two tides and sleep down there in a shed at Cotehele - I think it's the toilets now!" For two or three weeks of the year the salmon used to flow: "twas always good money… salmon was out of everybody's reach back then".

At cherry time he'd pick for Mr Cradick at Bohetherick Farm. Lots of local people helped with picking: "a chip for themselves and one for the farmer". He didn't enjoy climbing the ladders, "a long way up fifty bars… all the best cherries is right up the top".

.

Maud Maddock

"Great drops" (Loganberries)

Maud's mother died when Maud was young so she spent a lot of time with her father. He had four and a half acres in Coombe, Harrowbarrow, where he grew a wide range of crops including loganberries and lots of rhubarb, strawberries and flowers. Some of his daffodils still come up each year.

Her father and grandfather used to buy and sell produce from their wagon, calling at farms. They bought wooden barrels of fish and oranges from Cornish ports to sell. There was no running water on the site at Coombe so they had to draw water from the stream with their shire horses, Violet and Peggy. "We used to cut young shoots of gorse through a chaff cutter and then mix it with oat straw; that was fed as a chaff to the horses."

During the winter they chopped and sold wood. They also made holly wreaths. Maud's grandfather taught her how to do this using the inside of several reeds, shaping them into a rose which was then fastened onto the wreath, "a very old fashioned wreath". She still makes them for her family. They had pigs for the family and 2,000 chickens for eggs.

Her father and grandfather had both worked in the local mines - the Prince of Wales, Kit Hill and Gawton. Maud and her father moved to Albaston and grew anemones, potatoes and runner beans on the fifteen acres there. They sold a lot of these outside their house. For a number of years Maud worked at the Chip Factory in Calstock. Maud is now a farmer near Tideford and still owns her father's land at Coombe.

Fred Jolliffe, 1969 (Ellbridge)

Pillaton Parish, Cornwall

Agnes and Ronnie Wilcocks

"I have a cousin who was a florist in London. She told me she bought some flowers from Covent Garden (in the 1940s) and the name on the box was a Mr Cradick from St Dominick."

Agnes and Ronnie Wilcocks were married for sixty-one years. They met at Pentillie Castle, where Ronnie started work as a stable boy at the age of sixteen in 1930.

He became an extremely knowledgeable and skilled woodsman and worked there until he retired. Agnes arrived at Pentillie from London just before the war to work as a maid, soon taking on the post of cook. There was little money when they first married and they grew flowers and vegetables. "I sent to Liverpool - violets, daffodils and anemones." In the 1940s Agnes made £5 bunching *Prince of Wales* violets for Mothering Sunday. Sometimes flower boxes were lost and no money came back.

"Ronnie went to different market gardeners of an evening after work because wages were very low." He'd be at Alec Cradick's ground in Halton Wood at 6pm and by 9pm he'd have picked 1,000 one-pound strawberry punnets. He was also a skilled cherry picker, climbing twenty bars of a ladder before even reaching the branches. Sometimes "a decent picker could pick twelve pounds an hour". He picked gooseberries at Sargent's Field. "It was easier on a wet day, the thorns were softer."

Ronnie helped to prepare the gardens for Pentillie's annual Cherry Feast each July, until it stopped in 1938. Swings were hung in the Lime Avenue and tables and chairs set on the lawn. Children were collected from the local schools and taken to the castle for an afternoon of games and cherry pies.

Ronnie was known as "Bunny" because he had the job of loading up rabbits caught by the gamekeepers into a lorry at Paynter's Cross. He rode his bike everywhere; even if Agnes got a lift he'd always arrive on his bike.

(Chris Chapman)

Richard Harnett

"Cornwall, and particularly the Tamar Valley, has always come up with ideas to meet new challenges."

Richard Harnett was the last Head of Ellbridge Experimental Station at Hatt before it was closed in 1976 after fifty-seven years.

The growers tried to overturn the decision but were unsuccessful. An enormous amount was lost as a result including a huge photograph collection and ongoing experiments as well as an advisor to support the growers with horticultural advice.

As Advisor he remembers the tomato growers using cyanide on their heated pipes to combat whitefly: "the growers were taking all sorts of risks". In 1975 there were twenty to twenty-five tomato growers in the Tamar Valley largely in Calstock and Cargreen and one in Stoke Climsland, Cyril Reed. Countrywide there are now forty-five big units mostly in Littlehampton and Cardiff growing tomatoes. "In 1975 you'd get 100 tons to the acre of tomatoes compared with 200 tons today."

After the closure of Ellbridge Richard continued to work in the South West. His wife Janet meantime ran their small nursery at Pillaton. It was on the site of former heather specialists, the Rowan and Hawke families.

In 1988 Richard Harnett retired and he and his wife began to expand the nursery. By 1990 they had glass and gradually built up their four hectare glass and polytunnel nursery called Kernock Park Plants. It is very large and now sells fifteen million herbaceous plugs (young plants) and perennials to the herbaceous plant industry.

The Nelsons waiting to shoot their net, 1950s - see page 54
(Alec Friendship)

Botus Fleming Parish, Cornwall

Ernest Townsend

"At the end of April the valley was white with blossoms and people would come to see the beauty of it."

Ernest Townsend lives at Sladeland, a former market garden of fourteen acres, where his uncle Richard Summerfield was brought up.

His uncle blew up trees in nearby Ziggerson Woods clearing the land to plant fruit. An area alongside the gardens, bordering on Kingsmill Creek, was dug out so that barges could pull in and off-load dock dung.

Ern remembers watching cider being made by two horses turning the cider press in the barns at West Town Farm. The cellars beneath the barn were filled with thirty or so great wooden hogsheads of cider. His father, also a market gardener, grew mushrooms there and had a field of chrysanthemums by the barns. Boxes of pears were stored in one of the barns and sold off as they ripened.

Ern grafted new cherries using clay from his "Long Field". His uncle had grafted *Brandy Mazzards* for the writer Quiller-Couch. Ern remembers the sound of the birds sitting on the telegraph wires dropping cherrystones.

Each year they threatened the crop. There were acres of cherries "until I was about sixteen in the 1950s and then as they died, out they came". One year he fell from a ladder "picking apples on a very steep hill, up a twenty-six bar ladder - snapped in half, but I was unhurt". They also had "three acres gooseberries sent away in mawns up-country by rail".

In 1973 Ern gave up, the increasing competition from imports meant "you couldn't make a good profit". Gardening "was just hard work. One thing I didn't like about gardening was the weather…you couldn't plan your day or week, that's why I went into engineering!"

Elaine Nicholls

"Wonderful blossom, wonderful crop. We've made three barrels of cider this year!"

Elaine Nicholls, the daughter of Bill Summerfield and granddaughter of Stan Summerfield, still lives at the market garden they worked called Hodges.

Stan Summerfield was well known for the excellence of his fruit gardens. He grew raspberries, cherries, apples (making his own cider), plums, flowers and vegetables.

The Summerfields came to Botus Fleming in the 1800s as gardeners to Charles Carpenter of Moditonham House. They became established in the village and planted many of the orchards for which Botus Fleming became famous. They grafted local cherries - *Green Stemmed Rumbullion, Fice, Burcombe, Brandy* and *Sweet Mazzards*. In the 1920s there were forty acres of orchards and the village known as "Little Japan" had many visitors during blossom time. Most of the cherries were local Tamar varieties.

Elaine's husband Chris Nicholls has continued to plant orchard trees amongst the older trees. His particular interest is in growing old Tamar and Cornish apples to make cider. He makes this with another local orchard owner who has also planted up acres of apples.

Arthur Blatchford

"Grew early rhubarb - everyone ate it."

Arthur Blatchford is the youngest child of Reg Blatchford and Annie Summerfield of Botus Fleming. He and his brother Tom worked at Swiftaford Farm at Hatt, where they farmed and market gardened growing vegetables (spring cabbage and potatoes), tomatoes and flowers.

He can't remember having any serious problems with pests and diseases before the war, or that any chemicals were used until after the war. He grew half an acre of rhubarb "which fetched good money". It was the first fruit of spring and before the Second World War "everyone ate it".

The period after the war was very profitable for selling flowers before other growers got their stocks up again. He also used to make cider at the pound at Hatt, which was owned by the local landowners, Symonds. Arthur added beetroot to the cider to give it colour.

Peggy Whale

"Primroses - the hedges were white with them."

Peggy Whale is the only child of Ira and Catherine Whale. She lived in the lodge at Moditonham House until she was about twelve years old.

Her father Ira was a tenant of Captain Loam and rented the walled garden as a market garden. It had two acres of ground and there were a further two acres of marsh for Violet the pony to graze. She remembers being woken by the Doneys' market wagon clattering past as they set off for Devonport market at 4am.

The walled garden was well provided with trained plum trees. It also had glasshouses of peaches, figs and grapes. They had *Bramleys, Gladstones* and *Duke of Devons*, "the last apple to be picked in the season and very fine". All the produce was kept in the "marketing house".

Her father grew spring flowers such as *Pheasants Eye*, Old English Iris *(Iris xiphioides)* and polyanthus. He also grew a great many raspberries, gooseberries and blackcurrants. Her mother did all of the bunching. She also had to pick the raspberries and gooseberries - eighty to a hundred pounds a day - that went into the big wooden jam barrels from the Co-op. At the beginning of the season they picked into punnets, but the entire blackcurrant crop would "go for jam".

Botus Fleming was filled with cherry orchards and the school was empty in July, as everyone had to pick: "the lads all had terrific colds". In early spring Mrs Symonds of Hatt House would get local children to pick primroses to send to hospitals in Plymouth, "a cold miserable job".

When Peggy was twelve they moved away to a farm. Within a few years they moved to Trekenner Mill, Lezant, a smallholding. Here they had an acre of strawberries and grew irises and daffodils. Peggy hated market gardening: "I didn't like that job".

(Chris Chapman)

Edgar Doney

"Sweet Williams helped put me on my feet."

Edgar Doney was one of five children arriving at Bunny's House in Botus Fleming when he was seven years old in 1920.

The Doneys, having started off as tenants, moving on to a larger fruit farm and orchard at Pineapple, were later able to buy Maraborough Farm through "sheer dint of hard work". This was a farm of seventy to eighty acres, where they started farming on a larger scale. The older brothers went to work for local farmers while Edgar and his sister Selina worked the farm together after the death of their father until they both retired.

On Saturdays at Bunny's, Edgar and his brother Ern had to each carry a peck basket (forty pounds) of eggs and butter a mile over the field to the road where their horse and cart were kept. The butter was wrapped in cabbage leaves to stop it melting. His parents took it to Devonport market where they also sold poultry, fruit, flowers and vegetables.

At Pineapple Farm they had four acres of cherries running through the valley. Reg Doney, Edgar's older brother, was known throughout the parish as the best and fastest picker. Using thirty to forty bar ladders, often tied together on the steep slopes, he could pick 360 pounds a day. Edgar still has several cherry ladders. "I ordered that ladder brand new from Nicholas Striplin up St Dominick." They bought all their baskets from the Rogers. "Fred Rogers was a lovely man. You'd order something in the morning and they'd bring it over that afternoon - wonderful men".

Their apples were sold for cider despite being teetotallers themselves. Their mother Maria used to say "Cider is the ruination of marriage."

At Moditonham Quay, beside Pineapple, Edgar remembers the hustle and bustle of the villagers unloading dock dung from barges into their carts. On Saturday afternoons people rowed over from St Budeaux and, after a walk in the fields, came to buy fruit. The Baptist Party came buying cherries for six pence a pound. On Sundays their aunt rowed up from Saltash to visit them. The boys swam in the river. The Dutch bulb salesmen's visits by taxi from Saltash station were "a red-letter day." All the girls (Selina and her nieces) would eagerly gather round to meet the men who came once a year!

Dorothy Cloake

Dogbole Farm - "The house was in the middle of an orchard."

Maria Barratt bought this farm from the Symonds of Hatt at the end of the nineteenth century. They had six acres of gooseberries and cherries. Maria's sons Sampson and Victor worked with their sister on the farm.

Sampson and Victor had fine reputations for their produce, which they sold from their lorry in Plymouth market. They grew daffodils, anemones, raspberries, spring cabbage, rhubarb and gooseberries. The daffodils were all the old varieties, *Watkin* and *Emperor*, and came up year after year with very little intervention. The *Double Whites* were always popular: "it's a lovely flower". The wholesalers "were always after it". In the season they'd have three or four pickers.

When Victor was elderly and had retired to a neighbouring bungalow he would still tramp around the farm. In his seventies and unable to resist picking the fruit, Victor was found with a broken leg beneath a cherry tree.

Victor and Sampson's niece, Dorothy, was brought up on the farm, but "didn't like to climb the ladders. The *Burcombe* was nice and sweet, the branches were low so you could pick them." People would "come back to our home" to buy a chip of cherries: "everyone bottled fruit back then".

Dorothy married Arnold Cloake, whose twin brother was Jack. They were both market gardeners in Cargreen and built glasshouses next door to one another. Arnold specialised in chrysanthemums, tomatoes and lettuce. Dorothy still lives near her sister-in-law Amy Cloake.

Cherry ladders, Doghole Farm

Captain Kitts and the barge (wreck shown on p.10) which he sailed or poled to gather seaweed from local beaches for sale to local market gardeners (Mary Langman)

Bickleigh Parish, Devon

Picking at Louds Farm, 1939 (Mary Langman)

John and Gladys Pethick

"It used to be a picture this valley covered in blossom."

John and Gladys married in 1949: "we met at a dance at Tavistock Town Hall". They started working together at Woodlands by Tamerton Lake.

There were fruit trees right down through the valley under-planted with daffodils "all in rows". The daffodils suffered very little from disease, growing beneath hundreds of plum and apple trees. In 1962 John and Gladys took over Louds Farm. Soon afterwards John pulled up the apples, unable to sell the fruit and within a short time "the daffodils went - seemed to disappear". The land at Louds "was some steep" and John "put the steepest land to Christmas trees." He put in 12,000 trees one year, "we had it really good for a few years", since there was no competition.

At Louds Farm they "took on a lot of gooseberries, blackcurrants and raspberries. The women would rather pick gooseberries than anything. You could sit right down and get in underneath - few scratches."

"I don't believe you'd be able to sell them now - everyone made jams of gooseberry, plum and blackcurrant." Gladys "used to love picking strawberries". They bought their strawberry runners from Lionel Fortescue who ran a nursery at The Garden House in Buckland Monachorum.

John remembers the Brightman family who came across from Bere Ferrers by boat: "they came before the railway"(before 1890). They ripped up the land below Woodlands and up by the station "they had motes (root balls) up everywhere. They'd fell the trees and pull out the root balls with winches and sladaxes".

"The best place we ever had (to sell their produce) was Tin Pan Alley (Plymouth market); we only had twenty-four inches! You could really sell stuff in there - could sell anything, even windfalls! People would buy six pounds (of apples) at a time, six pounds for a shilling! We even had a big bath full of beetroot we'd carry in!"

John still grows plants for hanging baskets.

Ron Luke

"It happened by chance, we just fell into it."

Ron Luke is the eldest of nine children. His father Stanley was a dairy farmer until 1950 when he got dermatitis, which prevented him from milking. The ADAS advisor P G Allen who lived in Tamerton Foliot, suggested that he try strawberry growing: " you've already got nine children to work for you!" The land was clean with no disease.

Ron remembers as a child his mother would have their evening meal ready on the large kitchen table when he got in from school. After they'd finished, Stanley would emerge pushing a wheelbarrow load of strawberry plants and call out "Clear the table we're going trimming!" They had no packing sheds and so it was done on the kitchen table.

The strawberries were mainly sold to a wholesaler in Plymouth. By chance a customer called hoping to buy some strawberries. Those ready were for an order and couldn't be sold.

Stanley let the customer pick her own. "Seeing her absolute delight when she returned with far more strawberries than she had originally wanted, Stan realised that this might be a good idea and Pick Your Own was born."

The heyday of the "Pick Your Own" period was in the 1970s. "If the sun shone everyone would go to the coast, but if it was overcast they'd go to Luke's Fruit Farm." People had just started getting freezers and would pick buckets of strawberries to fill them. They had twenty-five acres of strawberries. In four weeks during these years Stanley earned more than his son does now in an entire season. Stan Luke went on to become a successful Soft Fruit Consultant travelling all over the country and became a Fellow of the Royal Horticultural Institute.

Ron and his wife, Hazel, along with their son John continue to run the Pick Your Own business, growing fruit and vegetables and selling produce from their farm shop.

Ron and John

Keith Langman

" My mother picked lily of the valley early in the morning. She bunched them and wrapped them in cones of glassy waxed paper to send to London."

Keith Langman's grandfather, J H Langman, came to Louds Farm, part of the Warleigh Estate, in 1914.

It was already a well-stocked horticultural holding of twenty-eight acres, as its opening accounts show: Daffodil - 2,700 *Watkins*; 2,700 *Emperors*; 3,500 *Barri*; 8,000 *Ornatus*; 72 *Bramley* trees, 32 on *Paradise* stock; 36 *Newton Wonders*; 247 unnamed varieties; 300 gooseberry bushes and one acre of four-year-old strawberries.

James Langman married Mary Florence (they grew a daffodil of that name) who was the daughter of William Rickard of Denham Farm, Bere Ferrers. They sold flowers to W H Press & Sons and Pankhursts of Covent Garden and bulbs to growers. Keith remembers fourteen acres of daffodils when he was young. They worked steep slopes going down to Tamerton Lake and almost all the daffodil acreage was beneath fruit trees. They never sent the bulbs for Hot Water Treatment and found they got very little disease.

Keith remembers his father, who continued the business, selling to Mrs Mock a high-class vegetable shop in Plymouth. She'd insist "sixty dozen lettuce must be fresh picked that morning". The flowers and some of the fruit went on the 4.35pm train to Waterloo from the station at the end of the road.

They had eight men and ten women working at the peak of the season. The men picked all the flowers, which the women prepared in bunching frames. Keith's mother grew lily of the valley in frames behind the house. These were packed into waxed paper and placed in boxes which, like the tissue and the raffia, all came from Fred Rogers. The packing shed walls were covered in certificates that they'd won in the Tamar Valley Flower Shows.

Landulph Parish, Cornwall

Gwen Ruse bunching anemones, 1949 (Ellbridge)

Amy Cloake

"Those Gladstones, they were lovely, shine like a dollar."

Amy Cloake comes from a St Dominick farming family. In 1950 she married William John Cloake, known as Jack from Cargreen. He had an identical twin brother Arnold who market gardened with him in the village. The Cloakes were one of the prominent horticultural families of Cargreen. Near Wayton Farm Jack and Arnold, along with their father, had six acres of ground fruits, raspberries and apples.

Behind their cottage Amy and Jack grew spot chrysanthemums from autumn till Christmas in a greenhouse. They forced daffodils beneath the greenhouse benches and also *Timperely Early* rhubarb. This was forced beneath black cloth tacked to the benches. They also grew lily of the valley in frames. It was very popular for wedding bouquets and for Helston Floral Dance.

Jack served on various committees and was on the board of directors of Calstock Chip Factory. He ran a sideline selling chip baskets mail order through adverts placed in "The Grower." He kept the baskets at Wayton Barn, Amy sending them through the post.

In the 1970s the land at Rosehill came up for sale at auction and Jack bought it. They built three huge glasshouses over five years using grants. The first went up in 1972 along with the boiler house and packing shed. They concentrated on one crop, all year round chrysanthemums, growing them in the latest high tech conditions.

Every Monday plants were flown into London from Kenya, arriving at Rosehill the next day. They were unpacked and put in the rooting unit. The chrysanthemums were planted every six weeks and the beds were picked every week. For peak times such as Mother's Day they'd have to plan twelve months in advance and have two units going instead of one. The flowers were mainly sold locally. They were the largest chrysanthemum growers in the Tamar Valley. Amy and her daughter continued the business after Jack's death until the early 1990s. The acre of glass is now rented by Kernock Park Plants.

Fred Billing

"The money was very little."

Fred Billing moved to Ellbridge in 1933 to three acres of land where his family made a living through the war years.

He and his father would take their pony and trap to Devonport Market. They had to walk, leading the pony up the steep sections and sometimes his father would even have to push. They would get the 4.30am ferry from Saltash. They took sixty dozen eggs each week to a butcher in a street nearby and they sold chickens as well as vegetables. At Christmas Fred's mother and sisters killed 100 Indian game chickens for the market. "They made a living on three acres".

At the end of the war the family "parted up". Fred worked on farms for many years and since he retired he has taken on Bill Cloake's old garden in Church Lane, Cargreen, where he grows runner beans, anemones and cabbages.

Gwen Ruse, (see page 113) Fred's sister, was one of the key staff of Ellbridge Experimental Station. She carried out research work on the anemone for many years. In 1972 Gwen was awarded the Royal Horticultural Society's Long Service Medal for forty-one years' service. Although she retired in 1974, she stayed on at Ellbridge working part-time until it closed in 1976.

Mike Pollock
"A job with a difference."

"I was involved in the challenges of a remarkably hardworking community producing these early crops and other flowers and vegetables, including tomatoes in greenhouses incredibly perched on the sides of steep hillsides. Soil sampling, diagnosing pests and diseases, suggesting, informing, grant aiding and always listening. Listening virtually without exception to a delightful group of experienced people - warm and friendly, full of good humour and admirable.

I can still picture my first advisory visit of all to Bill Rickard at St Dominick and his robust greeting that led on to enduring friendship. I recall the practical wisdom of George Brown, courteously listening with his chin on his hands propped up by a hoe. I can still see the smiling faces of Dan and Peter du Plessis and Stanley Luke, and hear the chuckle of Horace Richards. I remember the cautious alertness of the Cloake twins, the thoughtful questions of people like Douglas Richards and Alan Langsford. The dedication of the Rogers, the Davys, the Studdens, the Hunns and the Harris's.

I remember being accosted by lively terriers and by Bill Moorish's gander and I could go on and on....

A locality with a quite remarkable social and horticultural history. What a privilege to have been just a small part of it all!"

(Pollock)

118

George Brown and Mike Pollock, 1960s (Ellbridge)

David Goodchild

"One of the most beautiful sights in the whole of the West Country is that of the cherries in full flower in the sheltered valleys of the Tamar."

"I joined the National Agricultural Advisory Service in 1947 and was posted to Ellbridge. I was rather apprehensive since I had been five years in the army and felt that during that time I had forgotten much of what I had originally learned. However my fears were groundless. I was fortunate to have a very kind senior officer - Miss K H Johnstone - and I found the growers in the Tamar Valley very welcoming."

He was an Advisor between 1947 and 1953 and for him, as for so many Ellbridge Advisors, it was a particularly happy period in his career. There was a "wonderful camaraderie" between the growers. Some of the steepest gardens in the Tamar were in Brentswood. He measured those of Albert Reep as 1:1 and 1:2.

The main strawberry of this period was *Madame Lefebvre*. There were 500 registered growers and on open days 800 people would turn up at Ellbridge. The Tamar cherries were still being grafted and grown. Other varieties noted by David, who wrote articles under the pen name *"Bullion"* for the "Commercial Grower", were *Upright, Burcombe, Rumbullion, James Bullion, Drooping Willow, May Duke, Herod Red* and *Fice. Fice*, raised by Mr Fitz of St Dominick, was a glossy black cherry of great juiciness and sweetness and his favourite. The cherries were grown on the boundaries between fields and holdings. He set up some trials on these cherries using smaller rooting stocks but unfortunately the National Fruit Advisor dropped the scheme.

In 1964 David returned to Cornwall, succeeding Miss K H Johnstone as County Horticultural Officer.

(Peter Herring)

David Goodchild and Katherine Johnstone, Autumn 1948 (Ellbridge)

Mary Clark

"Dad had it hard."

Mary Clark is the only child of Kitty and Cecil Clark. Her mother's family farmed at Tinnel on the edge of the Tamar.

Mary remembers wonderful Christmases at Tinnel followed by a great Boxing Day rabbit shoot.

Her father Cecil, partially disabled in one leg, "loved gardening" but found it difficult. He started a poultry business but during the war feed shortages persuaded him to start market gardening. He took on four acres of the Glebe Field in Cargreen and sank a well, built packing sheds and a pigsty. They always kept two pigs, which they killed themselves each year. Kitty devised recipes to use every scrap of meat. They kept a few hens whose eggs were sent to the Egg Packing Station at Kelly Bray.

When Mary was twelve years old her mother Kitty collapsed by the by the side of the road. She'd had a stroke.

Kitty learnt to do everything with her left hand and was soon a skilled cook again, turning out "pasties as fine as anyone". Mary stayed at home looking after her from time to time.

At Glebe Field the work was hard although Mary and her father both liked using the rotovator. Mary's greatest dislike was growing tomatoes - the staking, wiring up the stakes, tying in the tomatoes, pinching them out, harvesting and grading them. They grew a wide variety of flowers including Sweet Williams, which she'd have to be up at 4am to pick. Well regarded by his neighbours, Louis Barrett said of Cecil, "No man in the parish could grow parsnips like him".

During the war Mary remembers the menacing drone of German planes coming down the valley. When her father was ill Mary had to run the garden and remembers bagging up cabbages for market, "heaving up the great bag to see its weight and finding it was ninety pounds!"

Her father retired in the 1950s and Mary continued until she married Ken Eastment in 1958.

Mary with tools made by her father Cecil (Chris Chapman)

Rose and Neil Cradick

"This is the first year we've picked cherries!"

Neil Cradick grew up at Lower Stockadon, Landulph, next door to Dulcie Stephens and her twin sister Monica who he remembers hurtling down the lanes on their tandem. His father Leonard George Cradick took on the smallholding, part of Pentillie Estate in 1933. They had four acres of strawberries, runner beans, plums and apples.

In 1945 they moved to St Anns where they continued market gardening along with farming. "We did a lot of *Double Whites, Golden Harvest, Soleil's.* Mother used to do the flowers." There was a cherry orchard but eventually they stopped picking when they "couldn't find anyone to do the work".

"We put up the first tunnels in 1972 and by the mid 80s had seven acres of strawberries, and one acre in tunnels. I used to love it, Marquands would load with a fork-lift 150 boxes a day, just to one wholesaler!

"In 1989 we got out of dairy because of milk quota restrictions. There used to be thirteen dairy herds in Landulph now there are only four. In 1997 we sold St Anns farmhouse with some land and moved to Tamara, and began trading as Tamara Soft Fruit. In 1998 we planted 700 cherries on colt rootstocks: *Colney, Lapins, Summer Sun, Sylvia* and *Sweetheart* all large fruiting modern varieties, and also two acres of walnuts."

Neil has sourced 300 cherry trees, *Regina, Celeste* and *Skeena* on *Gisella 5* rootstocks, for planting in autumn 2004. He is going to share these with two St Dominick growers, Nigel Hunn and Alan Rickard.

"We're back to 10,000 strawberry plants so we can manage. We're planting more raspberries where the sunflowers were. It's been a good year for strawberries, a good year for cherries and the best for raspberries."

Louis Barrett

"I was the first, I did all the spade work" - Mr Iceberg

Louis Barrett and his father both had careers in horticulture and farming in Cargreen.

In the 1930s his father had "a tremendous piece of asters that he could hardly sell". A button boy standing on the top of the display mast in Devonport Naval Barracks during the Navy Day celebrations fell to his death. "Hearl the florists at Devonport rang my father and took all (the asters) he had", as everyone wanted wreaths, "so my father did quite well out of a tragedy".

For Louis "the main thing in my life were two crops, kale and *Icebergs*". He would buy *Hungary Gap* kale from farmers and sell it in the market making a large profit. However very soon everyone else was doing it.

His career in *Iceberg* lettuces began when he had gone to deliver his produce to Plymouth market and on seeing some very small lettuce, three dozen to a box, he commiserated with the salesman. The salesman said if he could do any better to bring them in. The next Friday he delivered his first *Webb's Wonderful* to market. "You take off the leaves and you've got an *Iceberg*."

The salesman said they'd sold instantly and made four to five pounds: "fantastic money. We'll take all you've got". So started four intensive years of *Iceberg* growing. "I did one and a half acres a week, every week, planting 25,000 with hand labour." He made more money in those four years, which were ended by ill health, than at any other time in his career.

"I had the most fantastic four years!"

Michael and Martin Braund

"We are one of the few lettuce growers this side of Bristol."

"We did strawberries before lettuce, sent to Newcastle and Cardiff." Michael and Martin Braund started working in horticulture in the 1970s.

Their father farmed and to provide a living for his sons turned to horticulture, as less land was needed. Grants became available under the Horticultural Improvement Scheme. However the huge rise in railway freight charges meant it was impossible to make any money sending fruit away so they concentrated on selling locally. For many years they supplied Plymouth Co-op. However the Co-op now buys centrally.

"Father had some of the first polytunnels out here, they blew away." As polytunnels were refined they "reshaped the whole horticultural business". In the 1970s they started growing lettuce, buying their first blocking machine in 1978. The blocking machine turned out a million lettuce seedlings a year.

"Before the blocking machine all the blocks were stamped out by hand on a concrete floor."

Glasshouse growers from Calstock like John Bennett, Clive Potter and Fred Stephens collected up to 40,000 seedlings a week. Louis Barrett of Cargreen planted a trailer load a week outdoors. They still sell seedlings to local growers including one in Calstock who has just started growing Calstock tomatoes again. The Braunds "sell up to 1,000 dozen lettuce a week in the season from April to September". Supermarkets aren't interested in small local growers so they sell to wholesalers in Plymouth and Cornwall.

They also grow half an acre of strawberries on their seven acres at Penyoke. Recently there has been "more growth in strawberries than any other crop". They buy hives of bees from Holland to pollinate the 10,000 plants of *Elsanta* strawberries - "it's excellent" - which they grow early in the season under plastic. These are all sold directly to local shops and markets.

Michael and Bonnie

Martin

Bill Evans

"A little bit of ready money."

Bill Evans is the fourth generation of his family to have farmed Clampit Farm in Landulph.

His great grandfather worked it in the years before 1886. Much to the dismay of his teachers at Callington Grammar School, Bill left at the age of fifteen to start work on the farm.

Having begun as a farm of thirty-seven acres, it gradually got larger until it was seventy acres. It had two orchards of three acres; some of these were *Bramleys* and eaters whilst some were for cider. Collogett Farm close by had a cider press and Bill would watch his father making cider there. The *Collogett Pippin* is one of the old Tamar apples. It is a large apple that cooks to a pulp and was raised here. His grandmother, Mary Evans, had a stall at Devonport market where she sold butter, apples and vegetables from the farm.

Bill grew cabbage, runner beans and peas which he sold to local shops and to wholesalers in Plymouth. He and his wife Audrey planted half an acre of daffodils, *Helios* and *Horace,* "a white one with a red centre eye". These produced a few boxes a week which went via Saltash station to Pask, Cornish and Smart, Covent Garden and Spitalfields. He had one full-time worker for "twenty-five years without a cross word".

He recalls that St Dominick was said to be the wealthiest village in Cornwall.

(Chris Chapman)

131

Peter and Fay du Plessis

"Tamar Fire…"

At the end of the First World War Peter du Plessis' father, a demobbed South African soldier, moved to Lower Marsh Farm.

He took a job at the Duchy of Cornwall's Poultry Unit. When it closed he rented the farm, marrying a local girl Mary Spear whose father owned all the quays around Cargreen.

Peter's father planted eight acres of apple orchards with *Bramley, Scarlet Bramley, Newton Wonder* and *Duke of Devonshire*. Each autumn their barns stood four feet high with stored apples. When the local market declined for apples they sold them for cider until this too ended when cider was taxed and the orchards were ripped out. They also grew acres of spring cabbage, salad crops, soft fruit, spring flowers, stocks, zinnia, asters and Sweet William.

In 1943 Peter's father died and his elder brother Dan took responsibility for the family and farm.

In 1953 Peter and Dan started trading as Du Plessis Brothers. In the 1960s they began to increase the bulb business, becoming bulb farmers and breeders. They concentrated on selecting new seedlings, naming and registering them. They retailed these internationally.

Dan's greatest skill was as an exhibitor and breeder. He was Vice President of the Daffodil Society and a founder member of the CABGA (Cornwall Area Bulb Growers Association). He was awarded the Peter Barr Memorial Cup, which the Royal Horticultural Society present to the individual who has done the most for the daffodil industry. Another highlight of the brothers' career was the visit made by Prince Charles to Lower Marsh Farm.

By the time they retired in 1990 they had sixteen acres of daffodil bulbs and a collection of 800 varieties. Two of their best-known introductions are the varieties *Tamar Fire* and *Noss Mayo*.

Barry Richards

"Seamless Seasons, boring now."

Barry Richards' family have been growers in Cargreen for generations. They run a nursery growing alstroemeria and foliage (six acres of eucalyptus) and a wholesale flower business.

Horace Richards, Barry's father, was a well-known horticulturist and Chairman of Ellbridge (1965 -1975). He had two acres at Ivydene in Cargreen, including half an acre of glass. Horace's father and grandfather had barges and ran a market boat from Cargeen to Devonport. Horace enjoyed "doing all his own marketing, a way of life", delivering produce to shops in his Bedford lorry.

Barry was amazed to find his father growing over "ninety-three different crops" in 1968 including apples, daffodils, loganberries and forced tulips, "beautiful cherry plums… Mothering Sunday was phenomenal". Everything they grew would be forced for the day, several hundred dozen tulips and masses of other flowers. It took enormous skill to ensure this. It was the busiest time of the year, and still is.

Barry went into partnership with his father wanting to grow carnations. However his father preferred growing natural season tomatoes. "I hated tomatoes. I wanted to grow flowers!" In 1971 Barry and his wife moved to their present site and started putting up glass to concentrate on carnations.

In 1977 the Richards began growing alstroemeria as well as carnations and have been growing them ever since. A new scented variety is being developed and breeders are constantly introducing new strains. However growing one crop and buying flowers from all over the world means that there are no traditional seasons anymore.

Barry's sons Paul and Darren are running the business almost entirely. Barry is concentrating on his two and a half acres of ornamental gardens. "I've gone to a lot of trouble to find the old herbaceous plants that my parents used to grow. It's almost gone around in a circle for me".

Barry, Darren and Karen

Flower bunching at Louds, 1940s (Mary Langman)

Buckland Monachorum Parish, Devon

Daffodil pickers with a Ransom tractor, Champernownes, 1952

Peter Argles

In the footsteps of "the Daffodil King".

The distinguished nurseryman and bulb breeder E B Champernowne established 'Champernowne', a twenty-five acre nursery, in 1920. It was run in association with the renowned daffodil specialists Wallace & Barr based then in Tunbridge Wells. Peter Barr was known as "The Daffodil King of his day." At Champernowne's site breeding programmes and the search for new varieties of daffodils were carried out. The most famous daffodil bred here was *Red Devon* (pre-1943). It became very popular as a cut flower in the industry.

In 1945 Lesley Wates, Peter Argles' grandfather, bought the nursery but for several years after that E B Champernowne continued to run it. They produced bulbs for the wholesale and retail trade as well as shrubs, alpines and perennials. They also sent away cut flowers together with the other growers of the Tamar Valley.

They produced strawberry runners and the nursery maintained a presence in the area showing at Flower Shows. Gradually the daffodil breeding and growing dwindled. This may have been because the publicly funded Rosewarne was established to take on this role. In the 1970s they grew fewer and fewer daffodils, concentrating on shrubs and herbaceous perennials. They sold strawberry runners to growers, as did Lionel Fortescue of the Garden House, Buckland Monachorum.

In 1983 Peter Argles took over 'Champernowne' and has been running it ever since as a wholesale shrub and plant nursery.

George Brown's planting digger, made from a First World War entrenching tool

Bere Ferrers Parish, Devon

William Parken with his strawberry carrier at Ward Farm, c.1930 (Stan Sherrell)

Alan and Lucy Langsford

"When I was a little boy I wanted to be a Dutchman when I grew up."

Denham Farm lies on steep ground overlooking the Tavy. William Rickard of St Dominick carved it out of oak woodland at the end of the nineteenth century. Denham was one of the largest fruit gardens and up to 100 pickers from Plymouth were employed in the season, sleeping in two storey packing sheds built with hearth chimneys. The men and women were housed separately. Denham was a production line with pickers feeding the packing sheds. When boxed the fruit was collected and taken to meet the trains at Bere Alston destined for cities like Glasgow and Birmingham.

Alan Langsford's father Charles Langsford was brought up at Birchenhayes Farm, St Dominick. After studying Civil Engineering at Bristol, Charles returned home unable to get a job during the Depression. In 1933 he bought Denham where he concentrated on "earliness" as general fruit growing had lost its profitability.

"Horticulture was absolutely dependent on earliness - a week before anyone else." He concentrated on early potatoes and strawberries employing six full-time workers. He gradually increased the daffodil acreage and early on in the 1930s was one of the first to grow anemones.

During the war Charles managed the chip factory at Calstock two days a week. His greatest problem was finding wood for the chip baskets; he scoured Devon for Scots pine "even taking one from Denham".

"When I was a little boy I wanted to be a Dutch-man when I grew up." The bulb-salesmen "all wore suits, drove nice cars and didn't work outside on the land!"

Alan's great passion has been for daffodils. He belonged to the Cornwall Area Bulb Growers Association, CABGA, a cooperative formed to buy Rosewarne bred daffodils. These were released for sale when MAFF closed Rosewarne in 1989. There were 150 or so new varieties, "a small proportion of which will stand the test of time." Alan's favourite new bulb has been the *No 5,* which is now called *Cornish Vanguard.* He and his wife Lucy are still growing daffodils and irises and some eucalyptus.

Three-toed potato digger, used to rake bulbs

A small sclum, originally used for dragging manure etc. from a dung cart

Sampson and Martin Channon

"Flower shows, hell of a day back years ago."

Sampson's father came to Well Farm in 1921. His father grew up at nearby Lockridge Farm, which was famous throughout the valley for its fruit. He developed the fruit farm and had sixteen acres of fine gooseberries. At Well Farm Sampson (Samp) became one of the "biggest growers of *Double Whites* in the country. It was absolutely beautiful."

He grew six acres of gooseberries and a large number of strawberry plants. In 1968 they had their worst strawberry season: "A bumper crop failed to make the first high prices when it came into competition with other parts of the country. It wasn't worth picking." Samp had to throw 2,000 half-pound punnets away as the strawberries rotted.

They used to send their flowers away to London, Manchester and Birmingham but now they supply local shops in Exeter and around Devon. Back in the 1950s and 1960s there were a "terrific" lot of market gardeners nearby. In Tuckermarsh every smallholding was "market gardening."

Samp and his son Martin have had to cut back their daffodil growing because of the cost and lack of labour. When Samp was running the farm four full-time men and six women were employed. Martin works with his father and one part-time worker.

The Flower Shows were very important and competitive in the 1940s and 1950s. The Covent Garden wholesalers provided the cups and a great deal of prestige was attached to winning them.

Sampson with his vizgie

Martin

145

Schuttkacker Family

"Father bought his first piece of land in 1955."

William Schuttkacker and his wife are second-generation market gardeners and farmers at Battens Farm. They run this with William's brother Ian and also William's son Paul. William's father Irwin, a German POW, first bought some steep south-facing land where he grew strawberries and early potatoes.

In 1960 they joined the exodus from the steep slopes and went on to flatter land where mechanisation could be used. The cultivation techniques of the slopes were too labour intensive.

At Battens Farm they have a herd of dairy cattle and grow cabbages, potatoes, sprouts and swedes. They used to grow a wide range of daffodils. They produce annual flowers for florists, which they bunch in their old packing shed. New varieties come and go swiftly and many of the hybrid varieties are more vulnerable to disease and require more spraying than was the case in the 1950s.

The Schuttkackers still supply local shops and are one of the few remaining market gardening families in the Bere Peninsula. However, more and more of the small shops that they sell to are closing down.

Christine and Amanda

An Austrian prisoner of war's name left in a packing shed at Rumleigh

High Cross Experimental Station, Bere Alston

Pauline Eick

"Runner bean weather…"

Pauline and George Eick (a former German POW) married in 1951. "I still get letters from Germany - I have to get them translated! His family had quite a hard time of it - they were in the Eastern Sector". They began market gardening at Rumleigh on five acres belonging to Jack Langman and went into partnership with his brother Harry and his wife Thora.

"I remember Nemphos - used to dip the bulbs for the bulb-fly in. It was in a big concrete tank right by the shed where I was bunching. I used to have the smell all over me. Eventually the tank was moved to the middle of the field away from everyone. A cat fell in and it proved how horrible the stuff was. It damaged the nerves and kidneys I think - there was quite a bill from the vets! There was some blooming dreadful things we used to use. There was no knowledge of all these sprays and no warnings on the things. I always think my husband's illness was caused by them."

After the railways stopped taking freight, George had to learn to drive and built up a round of shops in Plymouth where he could sell their produce. This meant he had to get up at 5am to deliver their goods, but would be back at the garden by 7am. Mrs Eick took their daughter down to the gardens in the pram, keeping an eye on her whilst she worked. Her son still remembers having his afternoon naps in the wheelbarrow as a small boy.

They grew a lot of runner beans. It always seemed to rain for the runner bean harvest. It was a "horrible job" as it was impossible to keep the rain out of their clothes. Imports of French strawberries began to undermine their prices in Plymouth. "Our prices were all right until they came in."

They retired in 1988 when George began to suffer ill health. By that time there were hardly any other market gardens left at Rumleigh.

Douglas and Paddy Richards

"Polytunnels - it was a major breakthrough really."

Fred Richards and his son Douglas became well known throughout the Tamar Valley as "progressive growers" always adapting and experimenting with the latest techniques.

Fred Richards started farming pigs and poultry on land his father bought him at Bickham, his fledgling naval career having ended with the First World War. On marrying into a market gardening family from St Dominick, Fred followed their advice putting his pigs' manure to good use by growing strawberries. This he did with exceptional results.

At 500 feet the strawberries at Bickham were never early and in 1939 Fred bought a neglected holding at Rumleigh on a south-facing slope in a sheltered valley. There is no novelty in early strawberries now, but "used to be if you had early strawberries you could make money, good money. Nearly all our casual labour came from St Budeaux, thirteen to fourteen, came by train in the morning and back in the afternoon. They were delighted to be out in the country!"

In 1959 Douglas and Fred began to develop the prototype of the polytunnel. "George Allen (an Advisory Officer) he said what about thinking about making frames of polythene to force on crops. I spent two winters making them, each section five feet long and fourteen feet wide…making five structures each fifty feet long." The first crop of strawberries did badly because of poor ventilation. The following year this was solved and they had "a bumper crop." From then on they covered daffodils with it, followed by strawberries and quite quickly "other people started taking notice."

In 1976 Douglas sold Rumleigh to Plymouth Polytechnic. At Bickham he continued to grow certified strawberry plants and flowers. "I went back to Rumleigh about three years ago and came back feeling awful; it's all gone back, always clean and busy, now its dead."

Douglas and Paddy

Peter Brixey

"Still got Winston Churchill..."

Born on a two thousand-acre fruit and vegetable farm in the Vale of Evesham, Peter Brixey has been farming at Gnatham since 1976.

The farm runs along the shoreline between the Tavy and the Tamar. His parent's farm belonged to Smedley's and all their produce was sent off to the tinning factory in Evesham. Three hundred travellers would come and go picking each crop as it ripened.

Gnatham Farm has had a "continuous" thread of market gardening and is associated with local families such as the Hoopers and Bill Egglestone. It was known for its cherry orchards. "We got the old cherries, about six trees left. They got a real deep black colour, absolutely scrummy." Peter has planted new Morello cherries which will begin to fruit over the next few years. There are also small beds of daffodils left like *Winston Churchill*.

Peter runs a local organic vegetable box scheme and sells his vegetables at Farmers' Markets. He has organic beef, but it is vegetable growing that he really enjoys. He employs one full-time workman. He knows many former growers. "I've seen accounts of people in Bere Alston back in the 1950s making £1,500 an acre on strawberries and anemones. They were rich!"

155

Woollcombe Family

"My father's horticultural dream."

In 1929 Major Woollcombe left the army and, having a strong inclination to grow things, bought Rumleigh House for a song during the slump. He built glasshouses for forcing narcissi to be followed by a crop of tomatoes.

His children Richard (Dick), Rupert and Donetta soon became involved making boxes and planting them with bulbs. Both sons fought in the war, Dick becoming a pilot. At the end of the Second World War Dick returned home to help his father. Meanwhile Major Woollcombe's health had become so poor that he had to rent out the holding.

As the glasshouses were let out, Dick began experimenting with other crops, particularly apples. They were sold at a fixed price of five or eight pence for the premium grade. He under-planted the apples with strawberries. When the tenant retired Dick took on the glass again. The pre-cooling of narcissi had been developed making them flower earlier. A cold store was made in one of the outbuildings and pre-cooled bulbs were planted in the glasshouses in November. Once flowering was over they were sterilised and planted out.

Gradually, mobile glasshouses were acquired running on rails between two sites giving greater cropping flexibility. Pre-cooled bulbs would be planted in an open site and the mobile house moved over them when they were ready for forcing. It was moved on to a vacant site to grow tomatoes. Meanwhile the bulbs would die down naturally and when they were ready they were lifted by a mechanical-lifter. Chrysanthemums followed the tomatoes, being covered by the glass before the first frost. Dick's wife Phoebe and sister Donetta helped as well as several workers.

"Pick Your Own" became popular and, despite being off the beaten track, they attracted customers. They grew soft fruit of many varieties, producing over a long period. When the Woollcombes retired the holding was let out to a tenant. Since then it has been let as farm-land. The glasshouses lie derelict or have been incorporated into the farm.

Phoebe, Richard and Donetta

Stan Sherrell

"It was an incredible amount of work."

This lorry belonged to Stan's uncle Howard of Lower Birch Farm, Bere Alston, who had bought it just before the outbreak of war from Longbridge. He used it as his market lorry, carrying his produce along with that of Ada (Stan's mother) to Devonport market where they both had stalls. Ada, from South Ward Farm by the river, had a fine singing voice. Neighbours working in the gardens on the opposite bank of the river would call over, "Give us a song Ada!"

Stan used to take his father's raspberries from Higher Birch Farm to the station in a horse and wagon. The wooden carriages were stained with the red juice which seeped from the barrels. "It looked as though there been a massacre in those jam wagons!"

The work was all done by hand on the steep south-facing slopes. Nine men were employed full-time and six women. "Before the war an army of men would walk out of the village to work on their farms."

After the war many men went to work in Devonport dockyard, working on the land in their spare time. One evening Stan counted thirty-seven pickers in a two and a half acre strawberry field. When news came that strawberries from Lincolnshire had reached the markets the cry would go up, "Spaldings in - pick for jam!" The strawberries were then pulled rather than picked from the plants.

Stan's father Harold Sherrell continued until it was no longer viable, "digging acres of soil with a garden fork!" He eventually seeded the slopes and now they've gone back to woodland, "I don't want to see it any more." One of Stan's regrets is that he is no longer able to "eat in season".

The Sherrell family arrived in the area when Stan's great grandfather became a "hind", a farm manager, at South Hooe Farm. He, along with William Rickard of Denham, pioneered large-scale strawberry growing at the end of the nineteenth century in the Bere Peninsula.

Stan working on his uncle's 1939 Austin K30 1½ ton lorry

Harold and Arthur Stephens

"The better the apple the better the cider we reckon."

Harold and Arthur Stephens have been making cider in Bere Ferrers for over fifty years as did their father and grandfather who planted some of the orchards nearby: "most farms had one you know, back in they days."

They like sweet cider so they have *"Russets,* lovely cider apples", *Glass* apples and *Cornish Gillyflower* - "that's a beautiful apple, banana flavour". The cider is made in old brandy and whisky casks. Some of them are hogsheads (fifty-four gallons) and others forty gallon barrels. To make a hogshead of cider, eight hundredweight of apples are needed. At harvest time a forty gallon barrel would last about a fortnight.

On their one and a half mile of shoreline lies Thorn Point. This crossing was used by market gardeners from Cargreen (on the opposite side of the river) taking their produce across the fields to the station at Bere Ferrers. Cargreen villagers used this as their quickest route to Plymouth. The Stephens remember children from Cargreen coming across to get to their schools in Plymouth. Hoskins Agricultural Merchants of Cargreen regularly used to deliver supplies by boat or canoe to the causeway within five minutes of receiving an order from the Stephens. Sometimes they would even deliver to the field they were working in.

Arthur and Harold (Chris Chapman)

The Doidge Sisters (Vera Jackson and Kathleen Webber)

"My husband sometimes had to phone the station for an extra van to be put on for our strawberries!" (Kathleen)

In 1914 Kathleen and Vera's father, John Doidge, moved to Hewton Cottage. During the First World War much of Hanging Cliff Wood had been felled and cleared. John Doidge rented four acres of this land. He worked long hours clearing it of tree stumps and getting it fit to work as a garden. It was a south-facing slope dropping straight down to the Tamar. The land was very early and he was often the first in market with his early potatoes and strawberries.

During the 1920s and 1930s his wife Nora took their eggs, butter, flowers and vegetables to Devonport Market on the market boat. She boarded this at Holes Hole. At low tide the boat was reached by a wooden plank. On one occasion their mother's neighbour, Mrs Rogers, slipped and fell into the mud. The boat waited while she fled home to change.

They grew gladioli, Michaelmas daisies, lily of the valley, belladonna lilies, carnations, pinks, *Prince of Wales* violets and daffodils such as *Emperor* and *Flame*. The garden was so steep that peck baskets had to be firmly wedged into the soil to stop them tumbling into the water below. Kath and Vera remember bunching flowers in the evenings during the Second World War when the sky was as bright as day, lit up by the Blitz in Plymouth. Kathleen and her sister Constance both married in 1946.

Kath married Arthur Webber and moved to Lockridge Farm. On its seventy acres it had one acre devoted just to *Leveller* gooseberries. Kath loved its "sweet pale green berries." They also grew strawberries, blackcurrants and redcurrants as well as daffodils and other flowers. In the season they needed fourteen or so extra workers. One year their strawberries supplied a royal wedding feast. Constance married a market gardener and lived at Homefield on the edge of Bere Alston until they retired.

In 1948 their father died. Vera and her mother continued the garden until Vera married Richard Jackson in 1953. No one took over the land and it has slowly reverted to woodland.

Kath and Vera

163

Septimus Jackson

Septimus found the Tamar Double White and realised its potential.

Vera's husband Richard Jackson was the grandson of Septimus Oliver Jackson, a farmer from Clamoak Farm.

It is reputed that Septimus Oliver Jackson found the *Tamar Double White* (a "sport" of the *Pheasant's Eye*) growing in his hedges in the 1880s. He was so captivated by its heavy scent that he gathered some up, sending them to market. They were immediately popular and so the *Tamar Double White* industry was born. It took several decades for stocks to be built up and by the 1920s the Tamar Valley had become synonymous with the *Tamar Double White*.

Septimus and Annie Grace Jackson, Clamoak, 1904 (Vera Jackson)

Nigel Timpson

"Hewton Nursery - a growing success!"

Nigel Timpson bought Hewton Nursery in 1976. It had been a shrub and plant nursery since 1969, before which it was a market garden. Hewton Nursery has become one of the leading plant growers in the country.

They specialise in propagating plants from seed and cuttings, which they sell to the wholesale nursery trade. They have a ten acre area of 25,000 mother plants providing cutting material as well as a three and a half acre covered site. It is a very efficient operation using the latest technology including a water-recycling scheme that cuts the water bill by 70%. They have thirty staff, up to ten of whom are propagators, at the height of production.

It specialises in camellias, ceanothus, cordylines, phormiums and grasses, selling over 1.5 million plants a year.

Norman Grills

"One continual round of pleasure."

Norman's father, Norman Stephen Grills, and uncle Hubert came from Bohetherick in about 1914. They ripped ten to twelve acres of Lopwell Woods, planting strawberries and potatoes. In 1917 Hubert was killed in Palestine.

Norman married Caroline Maud of Hallowell Farm and went to live there. They had orchards of plums, *Early Orleans, Rivers, Czar* and *Belle de Louvain* that were planted in 1927 and cropped well for thirty years. Among their apples were red-fleshed *American Mother* and yellow skinned *Millers Seedling*.

Norman's family, including his identical twin brother Hubert, all moved to Hensbury, which their father had built. They farmed and also had daffodils, fruit and anemones.

For some years Norman worked with his brother Hubert who then went into dairy farming. Norman continued market gardening and farming with his wife Christine. In the 1970s during the electricity shortages caused by Heath's three day week they bunched flowers in the kitchen.

They always had pigs on the farm whose manure they used: "we liked to keep artificials to a minimum". He also preferred to spray the crops as little as possible. F R Roach, a National Fruit Advisor, carried out raspberry trials at Hensbury producing the world's record raspberry crop for that year. They had plots of new *Malling* varieties, *P* (later called *Promise*), as well as virus-free New Zealand stocks of *Lloyd George*. Norman bought his strawberry runners from Douglas Richards, "a very progressive grower".

After the railway freight prices increased in 1967 Norman began to sell to local shops and grew for the "Pick Your Own" market. He and his wife retired in the 1990s. He now breeds Rhode Island and Light Sussex chickens.

Iris Snell

"We used to go picking primroses before we married."

Iris' grandfather, John Down, was born in St Dominick in 1873. In 1921 he bought North Hooe Farm in the Mount Edgcumbe sale, which is on the opposite side of the river. When his son Horace reached school age his father insisted that he made the ferry crossing to school in St Dominick.

In 1930 Horace married May Parkin of South Ward Farm "quite opposite Cotehele". They moved to nearby South Ward Mine engine house, which the Edgcumbe estate converted into a house for them and there they market-gardened.

Her mother and grandmother Down travelled to market every Saturday on the market boat, the "Empress." They would wrap up pig's liver in cabbage leaves. They took strawberries, flowers and Kilner jars of cherries and "went to Devonport market right up to the day it stopped."

Iris' grandfather Parkin had point and dock dung unloaded at his quay to spread over "his gardens". They were "paid a premium" for their *Double White* daffodils by J & E Page of Covent Garden.

When she was three her parents moved to Helston Farm taking with them many of their daffodil bulbs and farmed there until retiring in 1963. Iris loves daffodils and remembers all the old varieties that her grandfather grew at South Ward Farm. Some of them still come up in the woods there half hidden by brambles. Iris is a skilled florist and after marrying John she continued working with flowers, bunching for local grower Alan Langsford. One year for charity she bunched 25,780 daffodils in twelve hours!

John Snell

"All the main cities were served."

In 1949, at the age of fifteen, John Snell started work as a railway clerk for the Southern Region. This developed into a lifelong passion for the railway and he has written and given many talks on the subject.

His father, like many other Tamar Valley men, went to Canada to work in mines in the 1920s. He ended up working at Henry Ford's plant in Detroit but was laid off during the Depression and returned home.

Some growers who delivered their produce to Calstock Station only grew one crop. Mrs Susie Burns of Dimson "made quite a lot of money four weeks of the year selling lily of the valley". Another was the flamboyant cockney Les Stone of Ferry Farm who specialised in beans on a large scale. At Christmas holly wreaths and pittosporum "went away". Windfall apples were sent in open wagons to Whiteways Cider. Cherries were sent away before 1949 and John can remember the last of the raspberry tubs being sent off to Robinson's jam.

The busiest time on the railway was the fruit and flower season. "Supernumeraries" were employed for the season with their offices in railway trucks. John "had to stack strawberries in pyramids on the handles of two-pound chips". The "perfume (in the vans) was really overpowering. I've seen the vans loaded right up to the top".

At Bere Alston station it was John's job to relay all the information about the produce loaded on at Callington, Luckett, Gunnislake, Calstock, Bere Ferrers and Tamerton Foliot to Waterloo Station. Here lorries would be sent to collect the goods and take them to the London markets of Covent Garden, Spitalfields and Borough. The goods would always arrive at the market by 4.30am but "Saturdays were always quiet as there were no markets on Sundays".

The industry died very quickly "when the railway stopped handling the traffic and reduced all the staff, they wanted to bring it all into Saltash and it faded away".

Flower boxes at Calstock Station, 1955. 400,000 boxes were sent away from Calstock, Gunnislake and the Bere Peninsula each year (John Snell)

Pop's shoes

Harvesting Memories:
Oral History and Market Gardening in the Tamar Valley
Kayleigh Milden

The Tamar Valley Service and the Cornish Audio Visual Archive (CAVA) have been working together to create an audio-visual profile of the history of the horticultural industry in the Tamar Valley. The aim of the project is to create a record of the knowledge, memories, and more importantly the 'essence' of local people who were involved in the market garden and horticultural industry which dominated many parts of the region for over a century.

Applying oral history fieldwork techniques has proven to be a rewarding experience for this community-based project. It is highly valuable in the ability to learn about the past and present from the people who are part of the social fabric of the local community and engages the community in the creation of their own history.

The ability of oral history to unearth hidden histories, to span time dimensions and 'give voice' to specific communities whose way of life has dramatically been altered by external influences has been a priceless asset to the project.

Over the space of a hundred years the landscape changed from wooded valley slopes to a patchwork of small market gardens coinciding with the rise of the industry, and then consequently reverted back to woodland after the demise of the industry. The vacillation between man and nature are, not surprisingly, even more relevant to agricultural and horticultural workers, whose socio-economic existence has been inevitably bound with the forces of Mother Earth. The decline of the market gardening industry has not only transformed the social and economic life of the valley, but the landscape and the way in which local people 'perceive' their surrounding environment has similarly evolved.

I hope this CD publication will give its audience an understanding and appreciation of what an important part these communities have in the history of the valley. Sadly we cannot include clips from every person that we recorded, but I would like to take this opportunity to thank all those people who kindly agreed to be interviewed for the project, all of whom have been so informative and welcoming. I hope it gives these people, in some way, the opportunity share their knowledge and tell their story, creating through these personal narratives their own history of the market gardening industry, which holds a very special place within the heritage of the Tamar Valley.

Glossary

All year round crop
Crops grown all year round instead of seasonally e.g. alstroemeria and chrysanthemums.

Baskets / Maunds
The peck (forty pound) basket was the commonest size used to hold vegetables, fruit and flowers: "Anything you had in the garden went into a peck basket" - *George Brown*. Many baskets were made locally by people like Mr Jago of Holes Hole. The Institute for the Blind in Plymouth also made market hampers, cherry baskets "held about fourteen pounds when heaped up" - *Geoffrey Mason*, gooseberry hampers, rhubarb baskets, etc. Market hampers had their owner's initials stamped on them.

Blind / deaf / deave
To produce abortive buds particularly associated with the *Double White*.

Brandis
A hollow three-legged iron stool used to cook on an open fire in packing sheds.

Brimbles
Brambles

J H Langman, Louds, Tamerton Foliot (Mary Langman)

Bucket
Galvanised buckets used to pick raspberries and gooseberries. Growers painted the insides with white enamel to prevent the acid of the fruit reacting with the zinc which turned the raspberries sour and black. Flower buckets were essential in the packing process as the flowers were given a twenty-four hour drink before being sent away. They were also used for forcing flowers.

Mrs Jolley bunching daffodils with raffia on a frame, wearing a bandage to protect herself from "daffodil rash", 1940s (Mary Langman)

Bunching
To bunch flowers and foliage. Before decimalisation flowers were generally bunched in sixes or twelves, daffodils in twelves, iris and calendula in sixes and small flowers (lily of the valley, primroses, snowdrops and violets) were in eighteens or thirty-sixes.

Bunching Frame
A wooden box used to bunch flowers in four rows of three. Growers generally used these for show bunches; however at J H Langmans, Louds Farm they used them all the time.

177

Butterfly
Double White flower which has half opened and half failed to open.

Butts
Bee skeps

Chip Baskets
Baskets with a handle made of planed wood and later cardboard. They were sold by Calstock Chip Factory and Fred Rogers and became popular in the 1920s. They were sold in gross or half gross bundles (144 or 72) of fourteen pounds (pre Second World War), twelve pounds, six pounds and two pounds. Tomatoes, apples, plums, gooseberries and cherries went into the larger sizes. The two pound baskets were used for strawberries, raspberries and redcurrants until the 1950s: "I remember this man selling us punnets, I couldn't get on with them and it was too much labour" - *Dorothy Start*.

Cold Store
An insulated temperature controlled shed / store to keep fruit and flowers cool and it could also be used to force flowers. It might be used to bring them on for Mothers' Day or conversely to hold them.

Cool Room
An atmospherically controlled room to keep fruit and flowers cool (pre refrigeration).

Coose

The area that can be reached by a picker from their ladder, approximately a six foot span. Sometimes it might take all day to pick two cooses.

Cornish Shovel / Devon Shovel

They were used to make "trones" (furrows) for planting beans and peas. They were also used for moving soft soil and turning the ground.

Crib

Morning break.

Daffodil Rash

Very common amongst pickers and bunchers, daffodil sap was thought to be the cause. People wore bandages in an attempt to protect themselves when picking and bunching. "Me face was plastered, I was covered but still had to do it" - *Freda Brown*.

Daver / Dabber / Dabberdy

Wilting particularly associated with lily of the valley. They had to be picked early in the morning to prevent it. Polyanthus were also prone to wilt.

Kathleen Langman bunching lily of the valley at Louds (Mary Langman)

An "earth car" at Brentswood (Ellbridge)

John Pethick's Earth Scoop

Dibber / Dibbler
This was one of the tools specially adapted to the steep slopes of the Tamar. It has a narrow blade set at an angle and was used for strawberry and bulb planting.

Dock Dung
Available for nothing in unlimited supply it was the combined rubbish of Devonport, Stonehouse and Plymouth. It was spread for years on the gardens of the valley until it was banned on the grounds of public health in the 1920s.

Drag hoe
Used to hoe strawberries that were hoed uphill on the slopes.

Drawing up Car / Earth Car
First made in Harrowbarrow during the 1930s. An old car was stripped down and a wooden axle attached to the drive from the engine. A wire rope was connected to the axle going down to the bottom of the plot where a plough or earth scoop was attached to it. The wife usually drove the engine while the husband ploughed uphill. Earth was brought back up to the top again in the scoops. Some growers used winches.

Dynamite
Used to blow up trees in woods being cleared for cultivation.

Eelworm
Attacks narcissus bulbs destroying them. Successfully treated with *Hot Water Treatment.*

Fertilizer
Limestone has always been needed on the acid soil of the Tamar Valley. Dock dung, shoddy, point stuff, bonemeal, and guano were also used. Cocoa waste and castor meal were popular in the 1950s. Growers introduced pigs or poultry to increase fertility. The tenanted farms were prevented from selling their manure, so growers found it difficult to obtain humus rich fertilisers. After the war many growers used "artificials" from the bag; nitrogen and superphosphates.

Forcing House / Hot Room
A packing shed/kitchen where heat was used to bring flowers into full bloom.

Grafting
The process by which two plants are tied together. The lower part forms the rooting stock while the top part produces the fruit and flowers. During the 1950s the saddleback method was popular. The graft was held in place with clay (dug from a field) and tied around with moss bound with hazel, willow bark or tape.

Gribbles
Wild fruit seedlings, which were dug up to form the rootstock for grafting.

Hoops
Bullfinches destroyed gooseberry buds and were shot until the Second World War.

Hot Water Treatment / Bulb Sterilisation
Invented by Ramsbottom who developed it at Wisley and in Lincolnshire. The treatment was commercially pioneered by Fred Rogers at St Dominick in 1928 and became the universal treatment for bulb eelworm. The bulbs were heated at a temperature of 110 degrees for three hours every three years.

The Rogers' Bulb Steriliser

Cherry picking, Brentswood, 1940s
(Norma Chapman)

Jowders / Jowlers
Hawkers came up from Redruth, Penzance and Camborne to buy cherries directly from the farms and gardens.

Ladders
The cherry growers all had wooden cherry ladders, up to fifty-two bars high.

Mash
Marsh.

Motes / Mocks
Tree rootballs.

Opes
Crops planted between widely spaced orchard trees.

P. eye
Pheasants Eye daffodil.

Packing shed
The packing shed was the hub of the garden. There children slept, clothes were dried over the fire, the main meals of the day were cooked and eaten, flowers forced and bunched, weighing and packing, flower and fruit boxes, punnets, etc. were stored. They very often had an upper storey where these were kept.

Packing house at Woodlands, St Dominick

George Brown's Dutch hoes

Patch hook
Used to cut and sharpen pea sticks.

Pitching thick
The setting of fruit, cherries, strawberries ("them's pitching") potatoes, etc.

Pitto
Pittosporum

Point stuff, point
An organic fertiliser of rotted leaves gathered from "points" in the river.

Polyanties
Polyanthus

Polytunnel
In 1959 pioneering work was begun by Fred and Douglas Richards on the development of the "walk-in tunnel". Ellbridge had their first walk-in tunnel in 1969.

Punnets
These were made from split veneer wood. The main sizes were one pound and half pound. Quarter pound punnets were less popular. Punnets were used in the nineteenth century, coming into use again in the 1950s when two pound chips, (for many years the standard container for strawberries), were only used for low grade fruit. "I used to like picking in chips best" - *Courtney Vanstone*.

Push hoe / Bush killer / Dutch hoe

"The wide ones for land that was planted with spring bulbs. The narrower was for hoeing between plants like strawberries. It was very light and easy to use." - *George Brown*. "They was known as bush killers as they were responsible for the death of many gooseberry bushes that were hit by it." - *Albert Wills*.

Raffia

This was soaked and used to tie flower bunches until the 1930s when rubber bands ('rings') replaced it.

Raspberry Tubs

The wooden tubs were filled with water overnight to swell the wood. Once filled with fruit they were covered with hessian tops and taken to the station or a pick up point. Locally the tubs went to the Plymouth Co-operative Jam Factory while others went by rail to Truro, Gloucester, Robinsons and Amos Hartley of Blackburn. The Tamar Valley Growers negotiated contracts with jam factories. At Bere Alston station they had a goods shed where tubs were loaded directly onto the trains.

Red Core

Soil borne disease caused by the fungus, *Phytophthora fragariae,* which decimated strawberry plants. It attacked the plants causing severe losses and became very widespread in the Tamar Valley.

Pickers at Bere Ferrers (Mrs Hooper)

185

Rip
To clear woodland for fruit planting - usually
with dynamite.

Scat
Split cherries

Scat forking / Shallowturn / Skimming
Lightly forking beds of strawberries etc., killing
weeds during the winter. "Winter work all we
used to do was skim - taking the weeds off"
- *Gerald Veale*.

Sclum
A manure drag. *(See page 143.)*

Scoat / Scold
Spreading manure usually done with a yule. A
winter job.

Seaweed
A fertiliser collected by those gardeners living
close to a source or with a boat.

Sladaxe
See *vizgie*

Soldiering off
This refers to the immature fruits forming which
go red and fall off if the weather becomes too
dry or too cold (the June drop). The word comes
from the red of a soldier's tunic.

The Rickards using their rotavators, c.1960
(Alan Rickard)

Spot crop
A natural season crop e.g. chrysanthemums

Stone Fork
A six- to eight-pronged fork used to prepare the
seedbed.

Strawberry Carrier

Many growers made or had these made to carry the strawberries picked in punnets. They held ninety-five half pound punnets and at cherry time, they held ten 12 lb chips.

Strawberry Planter / Planting Digger

This was a tool adapted from the First World War entrenching tool. "I bet there was a thousand in this village; they were such good quality" - *George Brown*, St Dominick. This was also used for bulb planting. *(See page 140.)*

Stringing Hook

Used for cutting strings of strawberries at the end of the summer.

Stroil

Couch grass, a real problem in the Tamar Valley where it was rife amongst gooseberry, raspberry and blackcurrant bushes.

Trimming / Pruning Hook

"Used to pare the hedges from November to February. Everyone did it, it was the winter's work" - *George Brown*.

Trones

Shallow furrows made with a Cornish shovel to plant peas and runner beans.

A strawberry carrier holding ninety-five half-pound punnets (Norma Chapman)

Daffodil pickers wearing "wrappers" (Champernowne)

Two claw / tiddy digger

"For digging up bulbs, hundredweights, tons I suppose in my day"- *Geoffrey Mason*. They were also used to break up the ground and for digging up potatoes.

Vizgie / Visgay

A double-bladed digging tool used to dig out trees. One blade was horizontal and the other was used for cutting roots. It was also used for filling in rabbit holes and for planting. *(See page 145.)*

Wrapper

Hessian feed and manure sacks worn as aprons and as wet weather clothes around the shoulders and waist. "When the rain streamed it was a common sight" - *Norma Chapman*. Manure sacks were particularly thick "put in stream, wash 'em, put up to dry" - *Albert Wills*. Washed in the winter they were stored in piles in packing sheds. Old UVECO sacks (filled with the maize flakes for cows) were very popular as they were big enough to go around the waist.

Yule / Evell

"We always called it a fork! It had five or six toes" - *Albert Wills*. It was used to scold the dung. The dung was piled into little heaps to rake out later. It was also used for turning the ground. *(See page 43.)*

Appendices

Raspberry pickers beneath cherry trees, Harrowbarrow (Mrs Pridham)

Tying celery, 1949 (Ellbridge)

APPENDIX 1
Some of the Fruit and Flowers grown

Fruit

Apples
Some of those mentioned in the text are *Hocking's Green, Blenheim Orange, Lane's Prince Albert, Worcester, American Mother, Bramley* (green and red), *Michaelmas Pippin, Cornish Gillyflower, Russett, Lord Lambourne, Millers Seedling, Collogget Pippin* (*Lawry's Cornish Giant*), *Newton Wonder, Duke of Devonshire, Beauty of Bath, Charles Ross, Gladstone, Box, Queens, Jubilee, Dr Harvey, Irish Peach, Vicar of Beighton, Ellbridge, Snell's Glass Appl*e and *Lord Grosvenor* (*No 1s*). James Lawry wrote that in the early nineteenth century apples "were principally (grown) for cider making". By the 1920s apples were being grown not in traditional orchards but with strawberries and bush fruit for cooking and eating and "the small sugar fruit sold for jam".
See '*Burcombes, Queenies and Colloggetts*' by Virginia Spiers for a fuller list of local apples.

Blackcurrants
Grown for jam for the Plymouth Co-op and also for market. *Boskoop Giant* (Dutch 1880), *Goliath, Baldwin, Blacksmith* (1916), *Laxton's Giant* (1946).

Cherries
Extensive orchards of small sweet mazzards were famous along the banks of the Tamar in the eighteenth and nineteenth centuries. These trees were very tall needing forty to fifty bar ladders to gather the fruit "almost every year some serious accidents occurred, often involving the loss of life and broken bones." *May Duke, White Heart, Brandy Mazzard, Herod Red, Best Black, Rumbullion, Early Red, Drooping Willow, Smutts* and *Jan James* were grown. The main Tamar varieties, which were hybridised and grafted around St Dominick in the mid-nineteenth century, are *Fice, Bullion, Birchenhayes, Burcombe* and varieties of these.

Jack Sambles' Burcombes, 1950 (Ellbridge)

Gooseberries

Early gooseberries were sent away and used in the dyeing industry. The main varieties grown in the Tamar Valley were *Keepsake* (1841), *Whinham's Industry* (pre-1850), *Whitesmith* (pre-1824), *Red Rough, Bottlestopper, Early Jenny, Gunner, Leveller* (1851) and *May Duke*. *May Duke* was raised at Topsham, Exeter, in 1900 and was a favourite for many years in the Tamar Valley which specialised in early dessert gooseberries. *Careless*, which became the most universally grown gooseberry was raised sometime before 1860. Gooseberries were used as a source of pectin by the jam and confectionery industries. In the early part of the twentieth century the demand for all jams, and in particular gooseberry and plum jam, was enormous. Dessert gooseberries were packed in hampers holding six to eight quarts covered with rushes and secured with hazel spears.

Plums

Small black plums were grown before the introduction to the valley in the 1860s of the *Victoria* (a cooking and jam plum, raised in 1840). *Czar* (1875) and *Early Rivers* (1834) were planted from the 1880s. By the 1920s *Czar*, an earlier fruiting plum than *Victoria* was the most profitable, "They richly reward the good cultivator."- *Lawry*. Plums were extensively grown for the jam market being much cheaper than strawberry jam. Plum and apple jam were supplied to troops in the First World War.

Rhubarb

"Everyone had rhubarb years ago" - *Albert Wills*. This was the earliest fruit crop of the year and growers aimed at having it ready for the Easter market. Early varieties included *Scarlet Cargreen* strain and *Raspberry Rhubarb*. A later variety was *Timperley Early*, which is still grown.

Strawberries

The earliest recorded strawberry variety in the Tamar Valley is *Alice Maud*. Another early variety was *Caroline*. These were followed by *Laxton's Noble* (introduced into cultivation in 1884), *Paxton* (1866), *President* and the legendry *Royal Sovereign* (1892). The early twentieth century saw the introduction of *Madame Lefebvre* (known as *Febe* or *Feebs*), *Huxley* (1912) and *Tardi de Leopold*. These, together with *Royal Sovereign*, dominated the early twentieth century until *Royal Sovereign* broke down with virus. *Madame Lefebvre* lasted until the Cambridge varieties were introduced. There was no other early variety: "*Madame Lefebvre* terrible taste, soft, went black and didn't travel well. We had women pickers here and even they didn't eat them!" - *Douglas Richards*.

The post war years were dominated by the Cambridge varieties, bred at Cambridge, all numbered at first and subsequently named. Of these, *Cambridge Favourite* became the leading commercial variety, although not in the valley.

Ada Sherrell, Eve Tremlett and Doris Portlock packing strawberries at Higher Birch, Bere Alston, 1950s
(Stan Sherrell)

Cambridge Vigour (known as *Vigours* or *C1*), "had everything going for it; early, good flavour and travelled well," - *Alan Langsford*. It was very popular in the valley. Other varieties were *Cambridge 422, 134* and *402*. A local strawberry "*Tommy Friendship*" was grown in Calstock for a period, a small but sweet fruit, which subsequently died out. *Redgauntlet* cropped well and became popular in the 1970s. *Gorella*, raised in Holland was also grown. The main variety grown today is *Elsanta*.

Raspberries

There was a large acreage of raspberries, often four to five acre fields, but this went into decline in the 1930s. The early varieties were *Thimble* and then *Beehive*, which soon became dominant. On four acre fields the *Beehive* yielded as much as a ton a day. *Superlative* (1877) and *Perfection* were popular. *Lloyd George* (1919) became widespread in the 1920s. In the 1940s and 1950s the Malling varieties created over a twenty year period at East Malling Research Station, became widely grown. The *Malling Jewel* (*V*), a largely virus tolerant variety, was trialled in Bere Ferrers and subsequently became very widely grown. In the Tamar, however, "We was all in *(Malling) Promise*" - *Albert Wills*. Varieties such as *Glen Ample*, *Autumn Bliss* and *Polka* are now grown.

Flowers

Anemones

Introduced to the area in the 1930s, the crop reached enormous proportions by the 1950s providing a winter income. "Anemones used to be a favourite 'cos they brought in the money" - *John Pethick*. By 1964 Philip Allington an Ellbridge Advisor told growers that they were making less than £10 an acre and in some cases "working for nothing". In the 1970s, the acreage had declined to 150 acres, due to problems with Downy mildew, corm quality and poor prices.

Daffodils

By the 1920s, the Tamar Valley was renowned for its *Ornatus* and *Double Whites*. Daffodils were sent in open flower up until the late 1960s (c1967) when wholesalers persuaded growers to send them in bud. Wholesalers J & E Page of Covent Garden lobbied hard for this change, stream-lining storage and transport, enabling them to build up an export market with boxes of fifty bunches instead of twenty-four to thirty. At first they were sent "goose necked" but this gave way to the "pencil" (seventy bunches to a box). Many growers still argue that the quality of the open flower was far superior to that of the pencil bud.

The valley specialised in *Narcissus poeticus 'Ornatus'* (introduced from France c.1870) and *Narcissus poeticus 'Plenus'*.

Some of the bulbs grown up until the Second World War were:-
Double White (c.1629), *Emperor* (1869), *Empress* (1869), *Grand Monarch, Grand Primo, Helios* (1912), *Horace* (1894), *Hospodor, Lucifer* (1897), *Magnificence* (1914), *Maximus, Princeps* (pre-1878), *P. Recurvus, Sir Watkin, White Lady* (1898), *Van Sion* (c.1620) and *King Alfred*: "There was never a yellow to beat it" - *Alan Preston*.

Some of the main daffodils of the post war period were;-
Actaea (1927) ("I was desperate to get hold of *actaea* - couldn't get any till 1950. It increased so fast, cropped like mad. There was so much in West Cornwall that growers were throwing it into the sea and then it became scarce again!" - *Douglas Richards*), *Magnificence, Carlton* (1927), *Fortune, Armada, Verger, Sempervanti* and *Cheerfulness*. In the 1960s, to these were added *Hollywood, White Lion, Golden Ducat* and *Ice Follies*.

Rosewarne-bred varieties became available in the 1980s such as *Tamara, Tamsyn* and *Martinet* bred by Miss B M Fry. With the exception of *Tamsyn,* these became the early mainstays of the South West's daffodil industry.

Narcissus poeticus 'Plenus', a sport of the *Pheasants Eye* narcissus, was known as *Double White, Whitsun lily, lilies* or *whites. Double White* sports naturally occur and have been found elsewhere and cultivated; in Lincolnshire in the 1850s and Middlesex in the 1890s. However it was the richly scented *Tamar Double White* that was the finest. It thrived in the valley but resolutely failed elsewhere. Its pure white flowers were wholly double and by 1920s the valley had became synonymous with this flower, as acres were grown. Some authorities think that this clone arose in the valley and may well have been found at Clamoak in the 1880s. It was popular for church decorations at Whitsun. Florists prized it for its intense perfume which no other flower had, something like the oriental lilies of today. "It was perfectly flat and pure pure white; ideal for wreaths and tributes. If someone died in January or February it was impossible to find a flat white flower (there were no white chrysanthemums until the autumn). The *Double White* came into its own in early spring." - *Terry Moss* . It became a chancy crop (in the 1920s Calvert noted that it didn't suffer from blindness) with a tendency to produce abortive flowers. It was one of the flowers sacrificed to meet wartime cuts of 75%. After the war most of the original clones were lost and it never recovered its former acreage. "One by one the growers stopped sending it."- *Terry Moss*. Once grown the length and breadth of the valley it has all but vanished.

Norman Preston picking tulips in Kelly Gardens, Danescombe Valley, 1940s (Norman Preston)

Iris

For a long period English iris was grown as well as the Dutch. In the late 1960s and 1970s the main varieties were Dutch, *Wedgwood* and *Professor Blaaow.* Combined with daffodils there were 400 acres.

Primroses

"The hedges were white with them" - *Peggy Whale.* They were gathered by children and adults alike for extra money. The peak of the season was usually Mothering Sunday, when children in cities bought them as posies. They were also popular at Easter. Children used the money for their Anniversary clothes and as pocket money. Some pickers were able to buy their wedding trousseau or holidays with "primrose money."

The Experimental Stations

Ellbridge Experimental Station, Hatt, Cornwall 1925 - 1977

This was established by H W Abbis on five acres of land, an acre of which was an outstation of the Royal Horticultural Society's National Fruit Trials. It served the growers of the Tamar Valley, running trials on crops, pests and diseases and giving advice to growers. It fostered the horticultural heritage of the valley and was run by members of its horticultural industry. Amongst its staff were Ralph Thoday, George Abel, E Beckley, F W Shepherd, David Goodchild, D J Fuller, J E Heath, M Penneycousins, Gwen Ruse, Christine Dunn, Neville Goodway, Philip Allington, Mike Pollock, Gerry Hayman and Richard Harnett.

High Cross Experimental Station, Bere Alston, Devon 1929 - 1953

This was run by the Devon Advisory Service. Set on a cold and exposed site, windbreak trials were carried out and experiments on crops including daffodils. The four acre site was owned by leading horticulturalist and farmer H W Sherrell. The building is still used by the local gardening club (see page 149).

Rosewarne Horticultural Station, Camborne, Cornwall 1951 - 1989

This Station was opened after the Second World War by the Ministry of Agriculture, to boost the horticultural industry. Breeding programmes were established for lilies, anemones, broccoli and daffodils. *Tamara* was the most successful daffodil. Ellbridge became a substation of Rosewarne and when Ellbridge closed it became the nearest horticultural station. The closure of these stations has resulted in growers being unable to get unbiased advice on the use of particular chemicals etc. Chemical and seed companies now dispense advice to growers.

A Field Day at Ellbridge Experimental Station, where the "Emery Rototiller" made its debut

APPENDIX 3

Advisors, Firms and Organisations

H W Abbis

H W Abbis was the County Horticultural Advisor for Cornwall for twenty-three years. He established and ran Ellbridge until NAAS (the National Agricultural Advisory Service) was formed. He did an enormous amount of work to promote the horticultural industry of Cornwall and the Tamar Valley. In 1947 he became Regional Horticultural Officer for the National Agriculture Service.

Fred Rogers Ltd 1910 - 1985

The Rogers family business served the needs of growers in the valley selling sundries, including Harvest Moon Binder Twine and raffia by the pound, through to DDT. They operated a haulage business collecting growers' produce and taking it to the station. They had the first bulb sterilizing plant where they processed tons of the valley's bulbs each summer and also operated a tractor contracting business sterilizing soil for growers. Fred Rogers was an eminent horticulturalist and public servant, who did an enormous amount for the horticultural industry of the Tamar Valley.

Ernie and Glen Braund, Horace Richards, Fred Rogers and Nicholas Soames M.P. at Ivydene Nursery, Cargreen, 1962 (Barry Richards)

'Starpack' Tamar Valley and Elburton Growers

A co-operative group started in February 1968 with thirty members to market and sell the produce on behalf of growers.

Tamar Valley Fruit and Growers Association c.1921

Started by a schoolteacher called Guy, with a motto of "One for all and all for one", this was a co-operative established by growers. By 1927 it had over 300 members and in 1953/4 over 600.

Plymouth Co-op Society jam tub

Calstock Chip Factory

The factory was established in the 1920s to make chip baskets and boxes for the horticultural industry. It was owned by the Tamar Valley Fruit and Growers Association and had a public bulb steriliser.

CABGA

The Cornwall Area Bulb Growers Association was formed in 1989, to bid for Rosewarne's bulb stock when the station closed.

Jam and Jam Factories

A huge growth in the demand for jam in the 1880s followed the abolition of sugar tax in 1874. Soft fruit acreage across the country rose from 36,700 acres in 1888 to 82,000 acres in 1907. Jam fruits were apples, plums, gooseberries, raspberries and strawberries. Most of the jam fruit from the Tamar Valley went to the large factories: Amos Hartley (Blackburn), Robinsons, the Plymouth Co-op, and in Truro and Gloucester. Small factories made jam around the valley: Kimberley Jam (St Ann's Chapel); Haye Farm and Woodlands (St Dominick), Weir Quay and other places.

APPENDIX 4
Flower Shows

The Tamar Valley Spring Flower Show (1927-1968) was established by H W Abbis to promote and educate the industry. It was held in March each year as a showcase for Tamar Valley spring flowers. Abbis strove to stimulate high standards in the industry demonstrating grading, bunching and packing. Wholesalers presented cups such as the Fenton Challenge Bowl, from Fenn and Hexton of Covent Garden, London.

Bere Ferrers and St Dominick had Spring Shows while Bere Alston and St Mellion had Summer Shows. These were big occasions with new varieties on display and providing the best growers with an opportunity to demonstrate their ability. "It meant a lot to growers as the big Covent Garden Wholesalers gave the cups. It always got back to them who had the cup and we'd get a letter of congratulation" - *Mrs Samp Channon*.

At Bere Alston Show the school was closed and there was a fair followed by a ball in the evening. At St Mellion cherries were amongst the exhibits either twelve or twenty-four to a plate. The largest cherries were used for showing. These grow closest to the trunk of the tree and were very hard to pick.

APPENDIX 5
Celebrations

Anniversary

Sunday schools held anniversary celebrations where children were rewarded for attending with games, prizes and teas. It was an occasion for new clothes and specially written songs and hymns. Anniversary was very important at a time of few holidays, when Sunday schools had a large membership. "When I was a child if you were a Methodist you were in!" - *Mrs Jope.*

Cherry Feast

This was an annual event at Pentillie Castle until 1937. Held in July, children were collected from their schools on the estate and brought to the Castle for an afternoon of cherry pies and games. The feast was revived and is now held at the Rectory, St Mellion.

Party Fields / Pleasure Fields

Successive generations of Plymouth Sunday schools and clubs flocked to the Bere Peninsula (there was also a field in Calstock) for their sole outing of the year. At first arriving by boat, and then from 1890 onwards by train, these occasions were the highlight of the children's year at a time when there were no holidays. "The tea was the wonder of the day", especially the tuffs and jam. Swing boats and games set out in fields in Bere Alston and Bere Ferrers, were named after the farm or farmer. Villagers sold flowers to the children. These trips lasted up until the 1950s and are still remembered nostalgically by the last generation to go on them.

Tea Gardens

Steamers brought trippers up from Plymouth to Calstock and Bere Ferrers to take tea in the fruit gardens or cherry gardens. Women in Calstock sold fruit to the visitors offering them tea in their homes. In 1860 the "Fairy", a steamer, was calling at "Mr Jackson's Tea and Fruit Gardens."

Ronnie Wilcocks (see page 86) on the two-ton "Field Marshall" - "It was the best thing after the steam engine for pulling - tremendous" - George Brown (Agnes Wilcocks)

Bibliography

Allen, Natalie, *A Stitch in Time,* (N. R. Allen, Lampton House, 1984)

Allen, Natalie, *Full Circle,* (N. R. Allen, Lampton House, 2000)

Booker, Frank, *The Industrial Archaeology of the Tamar Valley*, (David and Charles, 1967)

Calvert, A. F., *Daffodil Growing for Pleasure and Profit*, (1929)

Duffy, M. (Ed.), *The New Maritime History of Devon, Vols 1 and 2,* (Conway Maritime Press in association with the University of Exeter, 1992)

Ellbridge Archive

First Prize Farm - "The Farm Prize Competition 1890", *Journal of Royal Agricultural Society*, (1951), p. 812. (An account of J W Lawry's Farm)

Goodchild, D. J., "The Industries of the Tamar Valley", *Journal of the Horticultural Education Association, (1954)*

Goodchild, D. J., "West Country Cherries", *The Commercial Grower, (1955)*

Grigson, Jane, *Jane Grigson's Fruit Book*, (Penguin Books Ltd., 1982)

Hills, Lawrence D., *The Good Fruit Guide*, (Henry Doubleday Research Association, 1984)

Johnstone, K. H., "Horticulture in the Tamar Valley," *Agriculture,* 62, (1955), 123-9

Lawry, James W., *Recollections*, (Lawry family, 1925)

Merry, Ian D., *The Shipping and Trade of the Tamar River. Part One.* Maritime Monographs and Reports, No.46 (1980)

Pollock, Mike, *Horticulture in the Tamar Valley*, (1971)

Roach, F. A., *The Cultivated Fruits of Britain: Their Origin and History*, Blackwell (1985)

Rogers, Vivian, *Market Gardening in St Dominick*, Unpublished, (1997)

Snell, John, "Fruit and Flower Growing in the Tamar Valley", *Tamar: Journal of the Friends of Morwellham*, Number 24, (2002)

Spencer, Colin, *British Food: An Extraordinary Thousand Years of History*, (Grub Street, 2002)

Spiers, Virginia, *Burcombes, Queenies and Colloggetts: the making of a Cornish Orchard*, (West Brendon, 1996)

The National Trust, *Phoenix, Pheasants and Fortunes: the Story of Cotehele's Daffodils*, (2003)

Victoria and Albert Museum, *The Garden: A Celebration of One Thousand Years of British Gardening*, (1979)

Acknowledgements

Thanks to the many people whose patience, participation and encouragement have helped us. We are especially grateful to Christina Jackson who typed the manuscript, Virginia Spiers for her criticism and generosity and also to Vanni Cook, Cynthia Gaskell-Brown, Steve Carreck, Ioan Lewis, Stephen Russell and Tim Selman.

We are very grateful to all the contributors, many of whom were unstinting in their advice and hospitality, particularly George and Freda Brown, Norma Chapman, David Goodchild, Sylvia and Geoffrey Mason, Lucy and Alan Langsford, Gladys and John Pethick, Douglas Richards, Iris and John Snell, Stan Sherrell and Courtney Vanstone. Also we are very grateful to all those who lent us photographs and documents and to Chris Chapman. We would like to thank John Lanyon for his help and also Mike Pollock for letting us use the Ellbridge Archive, which he saved. Thanks also to Mary Martin and James Evans.

We are very grateful to Kayleigh Milden and her team of oral history volunteers who undertook the recordings: Maria Harrington, Mavis Kelly and Jill Lane.

We would particularly like to thank our sponsors: the Local Heritage Initiative, the Nationwide Building Society and the Countryside Agency.

Index

Page numbers in *italics* refer to illustrations

Abbis, H.W. 197, 198, 200
Abel, George 197
Allen, George 152
Allen, Natalie 20; *21*
Allington, Philip 194, 197
Argles, Peter 138; *138, 139*

Barr, Peter 138
Barratt family 102
Barrett, Louis 122, 126, 128; *127*
Beckley, E. 197
Bennett, Ivy *1*
Bennett, John 128
Billing, Fred 116; *116, 117*
Blatchford, Arthur 96; *96, 97*
Blatchford, Reg 96
Blatchford, Tom 96
Blight Brothers 80
Braund family 12, 64, 128; *129, 198*
Brightman family 106
Brixey, Peter 154; *154, 155*
Brown, Freda 16; *17*
Brown, George 16, 118; *17, 119, 140*
Burns, Susie 172

CABGA (Cornwall Area Bulb
Growers Association) 132, 142, 199
Calstock Chip Factory 60, 114, 199
Carpenter, Charles 94
Carter, Fred 64
Champernowne, E.B. 138
Channon, Sampson and Martin 144; *144, 145*
Chapman, Norma 40; *41*
Cherry Feast 46, 86, 201

Clark, Cecil 122
Clark, Kitty 122
Clark, Mary 122; *123*
Clarke, Joan 30
Clarke, Roy 12, 30; *31*
Cloake, Amy 114; *115*
Cloake, Arnold 114, 118
Cloake, Dorothy 102
Cloake, William John (Jack) 114, 118
Collins, Adrian 32
Collins, Gwen 32
Collins, Joe 12, 32; *33*
Congdon family 38; *2*
Courtis, Pop 44, 52; *45, 174*
Covent Garden Market 6, 9
Cradick, Alec 86
Cradick, George 60
Cradick, Ivan 30
Cradick, Leonard George 124
Cradick, Rose and Neil 12, 124; *125*
Crowell, Martin and May 12, 52; *53*

Davy, Douglas 58, 118; *59*
Davy, Kenneth 58
Devonport Market 6, 9, 158, 162
Doidge sisters 162; *163*
Doidge, John 162
Doney family 98, 100
Doney, Edgar 100; *101*
Doney, Selina 100
Down family 170
Du Plessis, Dan 50, 118, 132
Du Plessis, Peter and Fay 118, 132; *133*
Dunn, Christine 197

Eastment, Ken 122
Egglestone, Bill 154
Eick, Pauline and George 150; *151*

Elias, Alan 78; *79*
Elias, Ann 78
Ellbridge Experimental Station 46,
88, 116, 120, 184, 197; *35, 121, 197*
Evans, Audrey 130
Evans, Bill 130; *131*
Evans, James 36
Evans, Mary 130

Fitz, Mr 120
Fletcher, Claude 76
Flower shows 50, 52, 144, 200
Foot brothers 14
Fortescue, Lionel 106, 138
Frise family 42
Fry, B.M. 195
Fuller, D.J. 197

Goodchild, David 120, 197; *120, 121*
Goodway, Neville 197
Goss family 64
Grills family 168; *169*

Harnett, Janet 88
Harnett, Richard 88, 197; *89*
Harris family 118
Harris, Stan 38
Hayman, Gerry 197
Heath, J.E. 197
Heron, Chris *34*
Herring, Mr 26
High Cross Experimental Station 197; *149*
Hooper family 154
Hoskins Agricultural Merchants 160
Hunn family 118; *29*
Hunn, Nigel 12, 28, 124; *28*
Hunn, Wendy 28; *29*

Jackson, Annie Grace *165*
Jackson, Richard 162, 164
Jackson, Septimus Oliver 164; *165*
Jackson, Vera 162; *163*
Jago, Mr 176
Johns family 38; *39*
Johns, Gladys *34*
Johnstone, Katherine H. 120; *121*
Jolliffe, Fred *84*
Jolley, Mrs *177*
Jope, Mrs 56; *57*

King family 68; *69*
Kitts, Captain *104*

Lane, George 78
Langman, Harry and Thora 150
Langman, J.H. 110, 177; *176*
Langman, Jack 150
Langman, Kathleen *179*
Langman, Keith 110; *111*
Langman, Mary Florence 110
Langsford, Alan 118, 142, 170; *143*
Langsford, Charles 142
Langsford, James Dymond 20
Langsford, Lucy 142; *143*
Langsford, Reginald 20
Langsford, Stan 30, 54
Lanyon, John 50; *51*
Lawry, Charlotte 8; *7*
Lawry, James Walter 6, 8, 9, 11, 14, 56; *7*
Lawry, May 14
Lawry, Olive 14; *14, 15*
Lawry, Walter 14
Loze, Horace 76
Luke family 12, 108; *109*
Luke, Stanley 108, 118

Maddock, Maud 82; *83*

Major, Les 32
Martin, Laura 20
Martin, Mary 36; *37*
Martin, William 52
Mason, Geoffrey and Sylvia 42; *43*
Mason, Sarah 42
Maunder, Ned 76
Mock, Mrs 110
Moore, Tom 64
Moorish, Bill 118
Moss, Terry 9

Nanscowan family 46
Nelson family 54; *75, 90*
Nelson, Vivian 54; *55*
Nicholls, Chris 94
Nicholls, Elaine 94; *95*
Nilsson, Charles 26, 54

Parken, William 20; *141*
Parkin, May 170
Pauls of Harewood *63*
Penneycousins, M. 197
Pethick, John and Gladys 106; *107, 180*
Plymouth Market (Tin Pan Alley) 9, 42, 64, 106, 126
Pollock, Mike 118, 195; *118, 119*
Portlock, Doris *193*
Potter, Clive 128
Preston family *74, 196*

Reed, Cyril 88
Reep, Albert 120
Richards family 10, 46
Richards, Barry 12, 134; *135*
Richards, Darren 134; *135*
Richards, Douglas and Paddy 118, 152, 168, 184; *153*
Richards, Fred 152, 184

Richards, Horace 118, 134; *198*
Richards, Karen *135*
Richards, Paul 134
Rickard, Alan 12, 24, 42, 124; *25, 186*
Rickard, Brian 24
Rickard, Edward 44
Rickard, Joyce 12, 24; *25*
Rickard, Westlake (Bill) 24, 118; *4*
Rickard, William 110, 142, 158
Roach, F.R. 168
Rogers, Fred 12, 22, 28, 100, 110, 181, 198; *181, 198*
Rogers, Terry and Vivian 22; *23*
Rosewarne Horticultural Station 138, 142, 193, 195
Ruse, Gwen 116, 197; *113*

Sambles family 40; *191*
Schuttkacker family 12, 146; *146, 147*
Scoble, Alec 70; *70, 71*
Shepherd, F.W. 197
Sherrell, Ada 158; *193*
Sherrell, H.W. 12, 197
Sherrell, Harold 158
Sherrell, Stan 158; *158, 159*
Snell, Iris 170; *171*
Snell, John 170, 172; *171, 173*
Soames, Nicholas, M.P. *198*
Spear, Mary 132
Spiers, Virginia 36; *37*
'Starpack' Tamar Valley and Elburton Growers 18, 198
Start, Dorothy *74*
Stephens, Arthur 160; *161*
Stephens, Brian and Mim 64; *49, 65*
Stephens, Dulcie 66, 124; *67*
Stephens, Fred 64, 128
Stephens, Harold 64, 66, 160; *161*
Stephens, Monica 124
Stone, Les 78, 172

Striplin, Alfie *62*
Striplin, George 26
Striplin, Nicholas 100
Striplin, Richard 42
Studden family 118
Studden, Elsie *49*
Summerfield, Annie 96
Summerfield, Bill 94
Summerfield, Richard 92
Summerfield, Stan 94
Symonds, Jean 68

Tamar Valley Fruit and Growers
Association 198, 199
Thoday, Ralph 197
Thrower, Percy 60
Timpson, Nigel 166; *167*
Townsend, Ernest 92; *92, 93*
Trebilcock, John 80; *81*
Tremlett, Eve *193*
Trenance, Lewis 28
Trewartha, Norman and Elsie 76; *77*

Vanstone, Courtney 26; *27*
Vanstone, Margaret 26
Veale family 18, 68; *19*
Veale, Gerald 12, 18; *19*
Venning, Fred and Alberta 72
Venning, Mike 72; *73*
Vosper sisters 14

Wates, Lesley 138
Webber, Arthur 162
Webber, Constance 162
Webber, Kathleen 162; *163*
Whale, Ira 98
Whale, Peggy 98; *99*
Wilcocks, Agnes and Ronnie 86; *87, 201*
Wilcocks, Ruth 60; *61*

Wills, Albert 46; *47*
Wills, Rita 46
Wilton, Gloria 70
Wilton, Vera 70
Woollcombe, Donetta 156; *156, 157*
Woollcombe, Phoebe 156; *156, 157*
Woollcombe, Richard 156; *156, 157*
Woollcombe, Rupert 156
Worth's of Calstock 10

CD Track List

Track 1 - Vivian Rogers (2.39)
Track 2 - Natalie Allen (5.43)
Track 3 - Sampson and Martin Channon (2.46)
Track 4 - Mrs Jope (2.18)
Track 5 - John Snell (2.52)
Track 6 - Mary Martin and Virginia Spiers (2.50)
Track 7 - Peter du Plessis (2.40)
Track 8 - Vivian Nelson (2.54)
Track 9 - John and Iris Snell (1.55)
Track 10 - Pauline Eick (2.46)
Track 11 - Norma Chapman (3.21)
Track 12 - William Schuttkacker (2.02)
Track 13 - George Brown (1.12)
Track 14 - Douglas Richards (1.11)
Track 15 - Alan Rickard (1.12)
Track 16 - Stan Sherrell (3.14)
Track 17 - Gerald Veale (3.04)
Track 18 - Terry Rogers (3.08)

THE SOMERSET LEVELS & MOORS

Ken Fletcher

Published by
Somerset County Council 1991
Printed at
Acanthus Press Limited
Wellington, Somerset

British Library Cataloguing in
Publication Data
The Somerset Levels & Moors
    1. Somerset — Levels & Moors
    I. Fletcher, Ken

© *Somerset County Council*
1991

The Somerset Levels and Moors represent real Somerset or the "Sumer saeta" - the land of the summer people. Today's wetland scenery with its many interests is controlled by man. If the drainage pumps were turned off, large areas would be flooded for much of the year.

The area's history is coloured by people of strong character and tough disposition - the early man who lived off the marshes some 6,000 years ago; King Alfred; the Medieval Monks; more recent drainage engineers and farmers. They have all left their mark upon the area.

This booklet unravels the mysteries of the Levels and Moors, its making and its special, but fragile, wetland wildlife. Its contents aim to assist interpretation and make visits to the area more enjoyable.

Contents

Acknowledgements 4

Introduction 5

1 The Creation of the Landscape 7

2 Prehistoric Life 8

3 Events in History 10

4 Landscape and Scenery 12

5 King Alfred - King of Wessex 871 - 899 AD 14

Athelney Abbey
The Alfred Jewel

6 Flooding and Drainage 16

7 Wildlife 18

The Meadows
The Rhynes
The Willow
Birds
Animals and Insects
Fish

8 Farming 26

9 The Willow Industry 28

Withy Production
Basketry
Charcoal

10 Muchelney and the Abbey Estate 30

The Abbey
The Parish Church
The Priest's House
The Village
Midelney Manor

11 Wedmore and Meare 32

Wedmore
Land Enclosures
Meare

12 Peat Digging 34

13 Historic Churches 36

14 The Future 38

15 Places to Visit 39

16 Further Reading 40

Acknowledgements

The Levels and Moors comprise a complex area. Many studies, learned articles, books and papers have been published about its varied interests and I have obtained much information from the books listed in the section on further reading. The definitive work by Professor Michael Williams "The Draining of the Somerset Levels" and published in 1970 still provides the best detailed background to the area.

Working for over 10 years within the Somerset County Planning Department to produce a planning strategy and visitor facilities in the area, involved liaising with local people and officers of statutory bodies. Their specialist knowledge, skills and enthusiasm about agriculture, countryside, wildlife, water control, archaeology and the peat and willow industry has encouraged and helped me. To them all I convey my grateful thanks.

Mrs Anne Coate of P H Coate & Son, Willow Manufacturers, gave me the stimulus to prepare this booklet which has been produced with the assistance of Bob Winn of the County Council's Department for the Environment. I owe particular debts of gratitude to Geoff Roberts, who was responsible for the principal photography, and to Allan Boobyer for the graphic design.

Thanks are also due to Dr Robert Dunning for his guidance and historical knowledge; David Bromwich, the local history librarian; John Humphrey of the Royal Society for the Protection of Birds, Chris Arden and Lyn Jenkins of the National Rivers Authority; Kevin Gotobed of the County Library Service, Bob Croft the County Archaeologist, Russell Lillford County Historic Buildings and Conservation Officer and Steve Minnitt of the County Museum.

I am indebted to Stan Davies and the RSPB, Noel Allen and Pete Thomas for wildlife photographs, to the Somerset Rural Life Museum Photographic Archives and also to Frances Griffith for aerial photographs and to my daughter Mary for the wildlife illustrations.

Ken Brown gave valuable advice and read the proofs. Pat Pittard and Dot Amor undertook the typing.

Spring floods in West Sedgemoor — viewed from Red Hill.

Introduction

Within Somerset, in South West England, is one of the best remaining wetlands in the country. Generally spoken of as the Somerset Levels but more correctly the Levels and Moors, it has a unique flat landscape covering 250 square miles. Traditional farming has thrived in the area and has been responsible for maintaining and creating many habitats and conditions now important for wetland birds, plants and features. Yet it is a little known place even though it extends from the popular Bristol Channel coast to beyond Glastonbury in the east. It is also bounded by the Mendips, Quantocks and the Blackdown ridges.

Frequent changes in the weather are noticeable within the spacious countryside. Darkening skies, threatening clouds, shafts of sunlight, early morning mists all add to the mystery of the knolls, mumps and bumps which punctuate the flat moorlands. They were known to the early men of the marshes and are one of the fascinations together with the folklore of the Dark Ages, the tales of King Alfred and the influence and power of the medieval monasteries over the area.

Past events and the changes of the social order are complex. A glimpse at the story of King Alfred, the Muchelney Abbey estate, the pattern of historic change around Wedmore and Meare and also the flooding and drainage works are indicative of the intricacies of the Levels and Moors.

"The silver meadows".

West Sedgemoor in summer.

Water and its control are as important for today's farming and willow industry as for the many forms of wildlife and the protection of archaeological remains in the moist peat.

The Enclosure Acts of the 18th and 19th centuries resulted in the digging of the lengthy drainage and field systems on the moors. Such hard work is an accepted part of a local inheritance that has led to the tolerant but independent nature of generations of local people who gain a living from the wetlands. This can be recognised in the 16th century bench ends at Brent Knoll church. These show the symbolic hanging of the Bishop of Bath and Wells who had caused local unrest by purchasing land in the area.

The area is a place to explore and discover. Each of its many interests warrants specialist studies and much has been published or is described at Visitor Centres or Museums. If people who visit, live or work in the area or can influence its future are helped in their understanding and enjoyment of the Levels and Moors, then this booklet has done its job. The photographs and illustrations tell their own story. The qualities of the Levels and Moors are such that the area merits the feeling of "pride in place".

1   The Creation of the Landscape

Within the geological timescale, the characteristic flatlands of the Somerset Levels and Moors were created in recent times. For some 2000 years following the end of the Ice Age about 8300 BC, the area was an extensive estuary separated by a number of ridges and low hills. The sea gradually receded and by about 4500 BC an estuarine swamp extended through the area and was colonised by reeds. Silts and clays built up naturally to form a sea barrier and a fresh water bog was created. Into the semi-stagnant conditions fell generations of plants that did not rot but built up organic matter known as peat. By 400 AD climatic conditions had altered and although the area was prone to flooding, it was less frequent and the formation of peat ceased.

Today's landscape picture has been formed by man's efforts to control water across the peat moors with elevated river banks, indented ditches and rhynes. These enable the grasslands to be maintained which now form the basis of the traditional farming pattern throughout the area.

There remains a distinct difference between "The Levels" - a six mile wide clay belt along the coast with an elevation of about 20 feet above sea level - and the peat "Moors", which are lower than the levels, only about 10 feet above sea level.

Today's green moors cover layers of dark peat formed over 1000's of years.

2 Prehistoric Life

Artist's impression of Glastonbury Lake Village
By M Forestier (1910) — in the Castle Museum, Taunton.

These bronze axe-heads, bracelets and rings dating from 1000-1200 BC are part of a hoard found near Edington Burtle in 1854 — in the Castle Museum, Taunton.

As peat formed in the swamps and marshes it engulfed the work of early man and a wealth of material has fortunately been preserved. Man first moved here when marine conditions changed to freshwater swamp: travelling by log boat and by foot he would have hunted game such as deer, wild pig, wild cattle and wildfowl. Farming developed from about 400 BC with cereal - growing in clearings in the upland woodlands.

Wooden trackways were built across the swamp and many have been found in the Westhay, Shapwick and Burtle area. They were built at different times using various constructional methods. By ring-dating methods, it has been found that the earliest dates from 3806 BC. It is known as the Sweet Track after its discoverer. The track ran from near the Polden Hills to Westhay and was a plankway raised above water on a skilfully made sub-structure of poles and pegs.

Throughout the period 3000 BC to 300 BC numerous trackways were constructed. Hazel hurdles were used for a trackway across Walton Heath and a preserved panel can be seen at the County Museum, Taunton. A trackway known as the Abbots Way ran across the desolate landscape of 2500 BC and linked Westhay and Burtle Islands. Another trackway across Meare Heath was constructed similar to a railway line with sleepers spanned by oak planks.

The remains of two Iron Age farming settlements dating from about 300 BC were discovered in the 1890's by Arthur Bulleid. Known as the Glastonbury and Meare Lake Villages, the Glastonbury site was enclosed by a wooden palisade and some 90 small round wattle and daub houses contained about 100 people. The site at Meare was likely to have been usable only in the summer because of winter flooding and the dwellings were quite flimsy. The people of the lake villages worked a farming economy with fields growing wheat, barley, rye and vegetables. Cattle, sheep and oxen were kept and the villagers were skilled workers of wood, stone, clay, bronze, wool and glass.

Weaving combs
Made from red deer antlers and found during the Lake Village discoveries
— in the Castle Museum, Taunton.

Found by peat diggers near Shapwick in 1906, this dug-out canoe dates from about 350 BC. The boat can be seen in the Castle Museum, Taunton.

The Sweet Track (3806 BC)
This reconstruction has been built in the National Nature Reserve at Shapwick Heath.

9

3   Events in History

Environmental changes are likely to have caused prehistoric man to abandon the area. During the time of Roman occupation, sea inundation brought in silts and clays and a drier climate stopped peat forming.

The Roman army occupied England between 43-410 AD, establishing sea defences, ports, towns, roads, and villa estates. Ports were built on the River Parrett at Combwich and 6 miles upstream at Crandon Bridge where the present A39 bridges the Kings Sedgemoor Drain. It is likely that the wetlands provided some summer grazing with buildings located on higher ground close to the sites of today's settlements, for instance Chedzoy and Westonzoyland. Sea walls were built to protect low lying farms and salt was manufactured using saltern evaporation pools in the lowlands north of the Poldens.

Eventually life became insecure and valuables were often hidden. Finds on Shapwick Heath have yielded fine Roman tableware and coins.

Legends of the area tell how Joseph of Arimathea came to Avalon and built a church and King Arthur came here to die. What we know of the Dark Ages after the Romans is that hill forts such as Brent Knoll, continued to be occupied as settlements just as they had in Neolithic times. Fine goods were imported from the Eastern Mediterranean and North Africa.

Records of events exist for the 300-year Anglo Saxon period until the Norman Conquest of 1066. Hunting and the use of the Somerset marshes for hawking probably gave King Alfred the knowledge to resort to those marshes at times of threat. Section 5 describes his actions.

Decorated pewter bowl of 4th century AD from a Shapwick hoard.
Local ware probably using lead from the Mendips
— in the Castle Museum, Taunton.

Part of one of two Romano/British silver hoards (late 4th century) of about 125 coins found at Shapwick
— in the Castle Museum, Taunton.

Clay moulds used for forging Roman coins about 3rd century AD
— in the Castle Museum, Taunton.

By the 11th century about two thirds of the Levels and Moors was owned by the Crown or by the Abbots of Glastonbury or the Bishop of Bath and Wells. The church was to play a leading role in the efforts to control floods and reclaim the marshes. The Benedictine Abbeys of Glastonbury, Athelney and Muchelney were all dominant in their effect upon the landscape and upon the social structure and order. They rented out lands for farming, held fairs and collected tithes, fees and fines. Many ornate medieval churches express the skills and prosperity of the time.

During the Civil War the defeat of the Royalists at Langport in 1645 resulted in the Parliamentarians gaining most of the West Country. Burrow Mump at Burrowbridge provided a strategic garrison. The Mump is now a memorial to the men of Somerset who died in World War II and is crowned by an uncompleted church dating from 1793.

The Battle of Sedgemoor in 1685, the last on English soil, took place near Westonzoyland. The fighting was between James, Duke of Monmouth, the first illegitimate son of Charles II, and the armies of James II who had come to the throne on his brothers' death. A night-time attack to surprise the King's troops failed as a premature shot raised the alarm and Monmouth's cavalry were frustrated by a ditch called Bussex Rhyne. At daybreak the troops of the King attacked leaving 700 rebels dead and 500 prisoners were herded into Westonzoyland Church. Monmouth was executed, 300 followers hanged, and 1000 transported. The Bloody Assizes directed the distribution of dismembered and tarred corpses for hanging in West Country towns and villages.

Re-enactment of the Battle of Sedgemoor by 'The Sealed Knot' for the 300th anniversary in 1985.

4 Landscape and Scenery

Nyland Hill and Duck Decoy — Cheddar Moor
In the centre of the photograph are the earthwork remains of Nyland Hill duck decoy. This decoy pool is first noted in 1668 and had gone out of use by 1844.

The landscape of the Levels & Moors is made up of a series of "saucers" - the valleys of five main rivers, the Parrett, Kings Sedgemoor Drain, Huntspill, Brue & Axe and their tributaries as they open out into the coastal floodplain. Fingers of higher land, such as the Polden Hills separate the valleys giving a sense of containment to its otherwise open and expansive character. The effect is to create an atmosphere of isolation and remoteness especially during the mists and floods of winter.

Visited rather than passed through, it often represents a lost world away from the noise and speed of traffic. The area contains a distinctive way of life which together with the landscape has developed over the centuries from the interaction of land, water and man. There are few other areas in Britain where this process has had such a marked influence upon the countryside's form, its habitats and wildlife.

Within the flat pastoral landscape are river banks, drainage ditches, lines of pollarded willows, plus standing water and flooding in winter. There is a marked absence of buildings on the moors except perhaps for the occasional barn or movable milking parlour. With few hard-surfaced roads the main access to fields is by grassy and often muddy droves. The higher ground, seen from the flat Moors, provides pronounced landmarks; the church towers rising above the villages; the erect monuments above woodlands; orchards, and distinctive trees and farm houses with their group of barns and buildings.

The landscape also includes the detailed and smaller elements- the rushes, reeds and plants of the water-courses; the sedges, flowers and grasses of the meadows; the call and flight of birds; the statuesque heron; the animals; the insects; the sounds of farming and the pumping of water. These all identify with this unique wetland.

The Burton Pynsent Monument
Designed by 'Capability' Brown and erected in 1767 by William Pitt in memory of Sir William Pynsent who had left his estate to Pitt, reputedly because of Pitt's opposition to the Cider Tax.

Flowers of a summer meadow in West Sedgemoor.

After suffering terrorizing raids by Danish armies, Saxon Britain nearly succumbed. That it did not was due to King Alfred. His Kingdom of Wessex included Somerset where his estates covered uplands above the wetlands and also lands at Wedmore, Cheddar, Burnham and South Somerset. The marshes of Somerset were to play a critical role in his campaigns.

By the mid 870's the Danes had invaded most of England but a truce had been reached with Wessex. In 876 and 877 the Danes pillaged Wareham and Exeter and a new peace was sworn. However, early in 878 Guthrum surprised Alfred at his Palace at Chippenham and his armies were routed. Alfred and his followers hid in Somerset, seeking refuge and building a fort at Athelney - "The Island of the Princes" which was surrounded by impassable swampy marshlands. Its location is just west of Burrowbridge, by the present A361 road and a monument marks the site.

At Easter he left the marshes calling his troops to Egbert's Stone, the point where the three shires meet. After a fierce battle Guthrum's army was put to flight, and finally besieged at Chippenham for 2 weeks. Alfred chose to make peace.

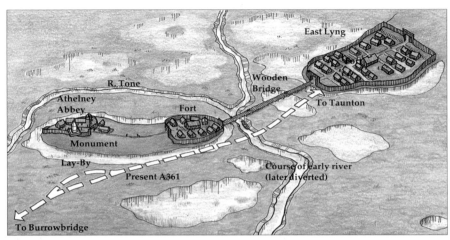

King Alfred's Fortress at Athelney 9th century AD
South of the present A361 - A fort on the Isle of Athelney was linked to another at Lyng by a long wooden river bridge. The river was diverted in 1154 AD and a causeway built (The Baltmoor Wall) upon which today runs a narrow lane.

Near Athelney at the Church of the royal estate at Aller, Guthrum and 30 of his leaders were baptised as Christians. Some weeks later the ceremony was completed at Wedmore and a Peace agreed. Alfred's fortress at Athelney was extended by a second fort at Lyng, being connected by a wooden river bridge.

Few Saxon people were literate. The King revived religion, learning and the rule of law. A history of the Saxons was begun - "The Anglo-Saxon Chronicle" - and most of our knowledge comes from this or his life story, written by his friend and priest, Asser. Many legends developed and some 200 years after his death the monks wrote that the King, whilst in hiding, took shelter with a cowherd. The man's wife left him in charge of oatcakes baking on the hearth and she scolded him for letting them burn!

Athelney Abbey

About 888 Alfred built a monastery on the island of Athelney. In 1534 it had an Abbot and 12 monks. Dissolved in 1539, discoveries show that it lay near the monument on the low hill.

The Alfred Jewel
(Photograph: Ashmolean Museum, Oxford.)

The Athelney Monument
Erected on the Isle of Athelney by John Slade Esq. in 1801. During restoration work, floor tiles of the monastery were discovered next to the monument's foundations. Note Burrow Mump in the background.

The Alfred Jewel

In 1693 in Newton Park near North Petherton, four miles from Athelney, an Anglo-Saxon jewel was discovered about 5cms long and 3cms wide. A gold setting holds a quartz crystal and it depicts a nobleman in coloured enamel carrying two flowers. On its border is the inscription AELFRED MEC HEHT GEWYRCAN - "Alfred ordered me to be made". A socket at its base, was probably for a short rod.

A study suggests the crystal was probably a Roman decoration from a wall or piece of furniture. It is housed in the Ashmolean Museum, Oxford who care for the similar - "The Minster Lovell Jewel".

It is believed that the jewels are from "aestels" or little pointers and may have been used to follow lines when reading a manuscript. Alfred had a translation made of Pope Gregory's book "Cura Pastoralis" (Pastoral Care) and sent a copy to his Bishops with an aestel. One can surmise that the Alfred Jewel may have been sent to Athelney Abbey.

6   *Flooding and Drainage*

Water has always dominated Levels and Moors life styles because the low-lying land is related to the sea and run off from surrounding hills. The slow moving rivers drain an area four times the area of the Levels and Moors. Flooding still occurs when flows in the rivers are high and water spills over the banks. They can become incapable of receiving water pumped from the low fields and also conditions are exacerbated if high tides in the Bristol Channel prevent discharge.

This wetland has given the county its name - 'sumer saeta' - the land of the summer people. In winter the people retreated to higher ground and used the land in summer when it had dried out.

Until the Middle Ages the lack of sea defences meant that really high tides would flow into the area. Bridgwater Bay has the second highest tidal range in the world and in storm conditions can reach 5 feet above the level of the coast. A disastrous sea and river flood in January 1607, said to be 11-12 feet deep, reached the foot of Glastonbury Tor.

It is suggested that sea walls were constructed by the Romans. In the Middle Ages a network of sea defences were developed by the Abbots of Glastonbury and the Bishops of Bath and Wells. These allowed the reclamation of the clayland levels, which being higher were more easily coped with than the low peat moors. The monks also modified the courses of rivers and built embankments in the Moors which helped contain floods.

Even so, by the 17th century only one third of the area had been drained. Attempts were then made by Sir Cornelius Vermuyden, a famous fenland drainer, to drain a large part of the moors. His efforts were, however, frustrated by the Civil War and the opposition of local commoners.

Southlake Moor under flood
A method of improving pastures is by warping the land - controlled flooding by river water containing silt from the uplands. In 1830 an Act of Parliament provided for Southlake Moor to be flooded for this purpose, a practise which is still continued to this day and in cold conditions can often form a frozen lake.

Westonzoyland pumping station
This pumping station, built in 1830 was the first of eight pumping stations built along the River Parrett to lift floodwater from the moorland fields.

Aller Moor Pumping Engine
Constructed by Easton, Amos and Son (1869), this two cylinder non-condensing steam engine worked twice a day during winter. It used about 4 tons of coal a day and was de-commissioned in 1955.

The Local Enclosure and Drainage Acts of the 18th century and early 19th century provided a new land drainage system. This changed the more rudimentary methods which had left much of the land in its natural state and subject to flooding and waterlogging. The Enclosure Acts required the construction of arterial drainage systems and the moors were divided into thousands of regular shaped fields by networks of rhynes and ditches. The commoners received their own small plots and thus originated a complicated ownership pattern.

New or replacement clyses or tidal sluices were constructed at the river mouths in the 17th and 18th centuries. A new river, the King's Sedgemoor Drain, was constructed in the 1790's from the River Parrett estuary into the heart of the area and reduced the risks of flooding. The introduction of the steam pump in Victorian times improved conditions by enabling flood waters to be lifted into the main drains and rivers.

During the second world war the King's Sedgemoor Drain was widened and a new river built - the Huntspill River - basically to provide water to an ammunition factory at Puriton. It enabled a vast area of the northern moorlands to be reclaimed effectively. Work also commenced on the replacement of steam by more efficient diesel pumps and in the five war years one third of the area which had previously been waterlogged was freed from all but the severest floods.

Of the five river systems today - the Axe, the Brue, the Huntspill, the King's Sedgemoor Drain and the River Parrett, only the Parrett and its tributary the Tone are open to the influx of the tide - to Oath lock on the Parrett and New Bridge near North Curry on the Tone.

The Mouth of the Huntspill River
Cut in 1942 across the higher levels, it extends inland to the lower lying moors and provides for their flood relief.

7 Wildlife

A succession of habitats evolve from the natural conditions of open water. Firstly the water is colonised by aquatic plants, then with the accumulation of plant debris and silt, the water gradually becomes shallow and turns to marshland. This is then followed by wet woodland of willow and alder with birch increasing as the land becomes drier. Finally the area becomes predominently oak and ash woodland.

This natural succession today is arrested by grazing and cutting coupled with the control of water levels and the marshes are now converted to grasslands or "grazing marsh". The open water fen habitats are now mainly found in the rhynes and ditches and in the occasional wet woodland.

Despite the enormous changes since the area was marsh and bog, grazing and hay meadows support a variety of plants and many of the original marsh plants, such as Ragged Robin, Kingcup, sedges, rushes and Marsh Orchids, have persisted where conditions remain damp.

It is the abundance and variety of plants that provide the basis for a diverse animal and bird life on the Levels and Moors. The wildlife - rich areas rely on sensitive land management.

Clearing ditches — an essential part of wetland management.

Southern Marsh Orchid

The best wildlife locations often flood for a few weeks every winter and remain damp with shallow pools in spring. Cattle are not pastured until after the eggs of ground nesting birds have hatched in late spring. Haymaking starts after the wild flowers have seeded and the butterflies and grasshoppers have bred. The wildlife interests of the rhynes remain when they are cleared over a 3-5 year cycle and their water levels are kept high. If not cleared they silt up and following the sequence of natural succession would eventually be covered in a scrub of birch, alder and willow.

The Meadows

Over 200 plant species have been identified in the meadows of the area. The richest unimproved meadows can contain 40-50 different kinds: however, 25-35 are more likely. The best flower meadows are those cut for hay and often contain the taller flowering plants such as Meadowsweet, Yellow Rattle and Yellow Loosestrife. Grazing pastures are sometimes tussocky and tall plants may grow and flower in the tussocks of Rush or Sweet Vernal Grass together with straggling plants such as Marsh Bedstraw, Meadow Pea and Marsh Birds - Foot Trefoil.

Occasionally orchids can be found and in May certain fields can be purple with Green Winged and Marsh Orchids.

A. *Yellow Loosestrife*
B. *Meadowsweet*
C. *Sedge*
D. *Sweet Vernal Grass*
E. *Yellow Rattle*
F. *Marsh Bedstraw*
G. *Ragged Robin*
H. *Marsh Marigold*

The Rhynes

Many plants of the rhynes and ditches are those of the original marsh.

Plants relate to the time cycle of cleaning, after which a gradual selection develop. First to appear are the floating plants such as Duckweeds, Bladderwort and Frogbit and next the "submerged" such as Starwort, Milfoil, Water Violet and Water Crowfoot. Pond edge or "emergent" plants then colonise the water at the edges and many are adapted as their stems and leaves contain spaces to carry oxygen to underwater organs. Plants with lance shaped leaves such as Arrowhead, Water Plantain and Great Water Dock push through the vegetation. As the rhynes become older the vigorous Bur-Reed, Rushes, Sedges, Yellow Flag Iris and Bulrush are established. At this stage it is time to clean again.

A. Yellow Iris
B. Bulrush – Lesser Reedmace
C. Branched Bur-Reed
D. Common Sedge
E. Clubrush
F. Arrowhead
G. Water Starwort
H. Water Violet
I. Water Plantain
J. Bladderwort
K. Water Crowfoot
L. Frogbit
M. Duckweed

Cutting the withy rods begins in November — hard, cold and wet work during the winter months.

The Willow

The traditional pollarded willow is perhaps the most distinctive tree of the Levels and Moors. The common Crack Willows *(Salix fragilis)* were planted to provide thatching spars and cheap hurdles and were pollarded or pruned out of the reach of animals. They were often planted along roads and droves to define routes across the moors in times of flood and by rivers and rhynes to help prevent erosion. They can provide shelter and nest sites for Little Owls and sometimes Mallard Duck.

The bark of the Willow contains salycin which is in aspirin and in the Middle Ages was eaten or drunk as an infusion to relieve headaches.

Cricket Bat or White Willows *(Salix alba)* are cultivated in the area and in 15 years can reach 60 feet (18m) when they are felled. Osiers or Withies, as they are known in the West Country, *(Salix viminalis and Salix triandra),* are grown in beds of up to 10 acres and in total amount to about 300 acres in the Parrett, Tone and Isle valleys. They supply the local basketware and charcoal industry

Pollarded willows — Tealham Moor.

The Curlew.

The bird life of the Levels and Moors range from species associated with open water, marshland and pasture to those of hedgerow and woodland. The seasons bring wintering, migrating and breeding birds but their numbers and success are indicative of prevailing conditions.

The moist soils in winter contain invertebrates near the surface. These provide food for flocks of lapwing and golden plover that fly in with

Male and Female Pintail.

Bewick's Swans on Tealham Moor.

cold winds from the north and east. At this time many redwings and fieldfares also arrive. When the moors of Somerset are flooded and conditions are severe in Northern Europe large flocks of wildfowl are attracted to the moors and use the areas of water. When disturbed, the wigeon, teal, shoveler and pintail provide additional whirling flocks to the lapwings which wheel across the winter skies.

Many Bewick's Swans spend winters in the same fields having returned from threir breeding grounds in the Arctic Circle. Visiting snipe are frequently flushed from long grass and tussocky ground.

In the summer breeding season, yellow wagtails are frequently discovered in the traditional pastures with whinchats and sedge warblers which nest in the taller vegetation. They migrate from Africa and join the busy reed buntings and the herons which nest in a few heronries in the area's woodlands. A well - inhabited heronry is at Swell Wood above West Sedgemoor and another at Midelney Manor near Drayton.

The Levels and Moors are noted for breeding waders - lapwings, snipe, redshank, curlew and a few pairs of black-tailed godwit but sadly their habitats have been reduced in recent years. They rely on food found by probing their beaks into soft surface soils which are dependent on the retention of a high water table.

An eel provides good eating for this Grey Heron. (Photograph: M W Richards/RSPB.)

Wigeon in flight.

The Marsh Fritillary.

The Hairy Dragonfly.

Animals and Insects

There is a wealth of animal life ranging from the otter to invertebrates such as water beetles. Their existence depends upon the conservation of unpolluted wetland habitats.

The area is renowned for dragonflies and damselflies. Insects are everywhere on a hot summer day and 22 types of butterflies might be found including the Marbled White, Small Copper, Common Blue, Orange Tip and Marsh Fritillary.

There are grasshoppers, spiders, flies, frogs, water beetles, toads and newts, many species of which are scarce or rare. Roe deer are widespread and foxes and badgers abound. The mink is frquently found and is considered a pest. It remains one of the areas in England where otters survive.

A few otters inhabit the quieter areas — but are seldom seen.
(Photograph: David Chaffe, Project Otter.)

Fish

The Ice Age made most British rivers uninhabitable by fish. Consequently, Britain has only 38 of the 5000 or so fresh water species. Most fish found in the Levels and Moors are typical of slow moving rivers. The gentle middle reaches and deeper stretches of water near the sea contain nutrients and the plants for food and shelter.

Bream and Roach thrive in the conditions of slow flowing waters. They swim in shoals, both species are fished in the Brue, South Drain, The Kings Sedgemoor and West Sedgemoor Drains and the Huntspill River. Indeed the Huntspill has a national reputation for Bream fishing. These and the majority of fish found here are of the carp family or are carp-like and include, Chub, Dace, Tench and Rudd as well as Carp. The Chub can reach 20 inches in length and is prized by anglers both for size and fighting qualities. It is found in the upper reaches of the Brue, the Tone and the River Isle.

The Tench are bottom-feeding fish. They inhabit weed beds and in winter become dormant, burying themselves in mud. They were introduced from Europe about 100 years ago and are found in the Kings Sedgemoor and West Sedgemoor Drains. It has been suggested that carp were introduced into Britain by the monks from the Eastern Mediterranean in medieval times. Carp like shallow warm water and are fished in the West Sedgemoor Drain where they can reach 24 inches in length. Pike and Perch avoid muddy and murky waters but can be found in the larger waterways, particularly the Kings Sedgemoor Drain.

Eels and Elvers are a product of the rivers. Eel and elver fishing is recorded in the Domesday Book of 1086 AD at settlements on the Parrett. The spawning grounds of the eel are in the Sargasso Sea off Bermuda - The eel larvae cross the Atlantic and after changing into elvers move up the rivers. They spend most of their life as yellow eels but after 8-12 years reach sexual maturity and as silver eels migrate on the Autumn floods to return to their birthplace.

Roach
The deep weedy rivers within the Levels and Moors provide ideal conditions for this freshwater fish.
— Photographed at the British Water Zoo, Cheddar.

Elver fishing on the River Parrett.

Vast tracts of open marsh, lake and wet woodlands would have been daunting to early man and his efforts to farm. The earliest evidence of farming on the wetlands is of works undertaken by the Romans within the claylands near Brent and also in the Axe valley. As the centuries passed, gradual and piecemeal reclamation and lowering of water tables allowed grazing in summer periods.

Farming progress followed flood-relief and artificial drainage work. Schemes and improved techniques since the late 17th century have almost completed the change from natural conditions. The general scene is now one of peaceful pastureland and it is difficult to appreciate that the area is man made for if the pumps serving the low lying moors were turned off, the land would be under water for much of the time.

The farming system which has evolved reflects the characteristics of farmsteads and settlements on the higher ground above floodable land, the problems of drainage and a fragmented pattern of land ownership. Traditionally the Levels and Moors have been devoted to livestock using the good growths of summer grass. Today's farming still simulates the traditional practices

and stock are usually overwintered on the higher lands in or near buildings. In the summer the grass on the moors is often made into hay or grazed by cattle. Dairy herds are frequently milked in portable milking bails in the fields. Sheep farming is now more widespread and reflects lower demands for dairy and beef products.

The rivers and watercourses function together and provide an essential base for farming within fields enclosed by a lattice-work of rhynes

or ditches. These rhynes - pronounced "reens" - are seen by farmers as "wet fences" marking the boundaries between fields and providing drinking water for cattle. Essential for moving the flood waters they may be penned to maintain high water tables which are important for healthy growing conditions in the summer.

The harsh conditions and traditional styles have created a fiercely independent people suspicious of change. The economies of modern

Milking at a milking bale in a moorland field.

farming have however led to a more intensive production on some land and further changes are possible. Deepened ditches and piped field drainage linked to pumps can enable larger fields to be farmed for longer grazing periods. Reseeded with modern ley grasses, these fields can increase production and support more cattle. Such farming developments in the landscape of the Levels and Moors are often criticised as being unsympathetic to the wetland landscape and its wildlife.

However a continuation of traditional farming is essential to maintain the area's landscape and wildlife heritage.

Cider, teasles, fish, eels and elvers are associated traditionally as products of the area. Teasles, traditionally used for combing wool, are now confined to a small area in West Sedgemoor but the catching of eels and elvers is a popular seasonal activity particularly on the River Parrett.

Big bale silage – Efficient farming but sometimes criticised as being insensitive to wetland wildlife.

Inspecting the teasle crop.

Cider orchards, a distinctive Somerset feature, can still be found in the area.

9 *The Willow Industry*

Withy Production

For centuries the strong flexible stalks of willows have provided stems for basket making. Osiers are shrubs rather than trees and a common variety grown is the Somerset Black Maul. Each year plants are cut back to ground level and in consequence the stumps, or stools produce many long straight shoots.

Each acre of willow bed can comprise 16,000-17,000 plants and with care they remain productive for up to 25 years. Their harvest begins in November and the withies are cut mainly by a traditional hand hook. Withies are processed according to the finish required. Boiling in water for about 9 hours prior to removing or stripping the bark produces buff rods. Brown rods are those where the bark is left untouched, and white rods are obtained by stripping live shoots of withies cut in the New Year. These are left to stand in about 6 inches (150 cm) of water and stripped in May or June when the sap has risen and the bark no longer adheres.

The industry was once more extensive and old withy works can often be detected from the tall brick chimneys extending from old boilers.

Basket making — using skills developed by generations of craft workers.

Charcoal being sorted according to thickness.

Charcoal

Artists' charcoal from the area is extensively exported and supplies the majority of the UK. demands. Prepared willow rods are cut to lengths of differing thicknesses then packed tightly in metal boxes about 6 inches (150 cm) square, ensuring air is excluded . These are placed in kilns and then fired at a very high temperature. Care must be taken to exclude air from the boxes otherwise the charcoal can be shattered by the explosion of expanded air. Once cool the charcoal is ready for use.

Basketry

A basket maker requires adequate space to work with willow rods of up to 8 feet long. The craftsman sits on the floor upon a sloping plank or lapboard with his back to a wall and the basket is inclined away from him. The buff and white rods are soaked for about an hour or so and left overnight to mellow or become supple and easy to use. Brown rods are steamed for 2 hours, or

alternatively they can be soaked for about 5 days.

Baskets comprise basically a framework of stems interlaced by rods. Successful making requires craft skills to control the rods, prevent kinks and obtain a strong and good shaped basket. The willow workers produce a range of products which include shopping, log and animal baskets, trays, hampers and chairs and tables.

Artists' charcoal ready for packing.

29

10 Muchelney and the Abbey Estate

Part of the Medieval ruins of Muchelney Abbey. The Saxon church of the first monastery stood in the central sunken area.

The Abbey

Once standing dominantly just over a mile south of Langport was the Abbey of Muchelney. Founded in the 8th century on an island in the marshes, it was surrendered to the Crown in 1538. A survey soon afterwards states it was a large and fine structure. There remains today the splendid Abbot's lodgings, cloisters, reredorter and exposed foundations with the associated Parish Church, Priests' House, barns and medieval village.

The Abbey estate included the three islands of Muchelney, Midelney and Thorney ('ney' means island), Ilminster, Drayton and beyond. Although having no more than 20 monks, it prospered from rents, fines, fees and tithes. Maintaining an enjoyable lifestyle, the monks had a summer retreat at Midelney which had a deer park and a pack of hounds for hunting. Costs of rebuilding plus the wages of servants and payments to keep friends in government and royal circles brought bankruptcy and surrender to the Crown. The King granted the property to his brother-in-law, Edward Seymour later Duke of Somerset but the Crown recovered it on his execution.

The Parish Church

Originally adjoining the Abbey which owned the living, it is of late Perpendicular style, containing a wagon roof adorned with an early 17th century painting of Angels and cherubs in Tudor costume. Patterned tiles from the Abbey have been re-used in the sanctuary and by the font.

The Priest's House

Close to the church, it was built in 1308 for the vicar and is a rare survival of an open-roofed hall house with rooms at both ends. A floor and fireplace were inserted in 1550. It is now owned by the National Trust. The cross nearby is thought to mark the site of two annual fairs.

The Village

Muchelney's southern village centre has pleasant 17th century houses and cottages containing fragments from the Abbey.

Midelney Manor

This Elizabethan Manor House is on the site of the retreat of the Abbots of Muchelney whose Abbey was some two miles eastwards across the deer park and the flat landscape. The manor house has been in the continuous ownership of the

Trevilian family, originally stewards to the Abbots. It has an insular and enchanting atmosphere, reflecting its isolation during times of flood. A rarity is the Falcons' Mews where the birds were tethered while they moulted.

Medieval floor tile depicting a heron fishing — found in the Muchelney Abbey ruins.

Fireplace in the Abbot's Chamber at Muchelney Abbey — said to be the most sumptuous 16th century fireplace in the Country.

Midelney Manor.

11   Wedmore and Meare

Looking north from the Polden Hills towards the Mendips, the Isle of Wedmore is seen surrounded by open moor. From here Neolithic man built trackways across the marshes and near Meare was a large Iron Age lake village.

Wedmore

The Saxon Kings maintained a Royal Estate at Wedmore extending towards Cheddar where foundations of a Royal Palace have been discovered. In 878 AD King Alfred entertained the vanquished Danes at Wedmore for twelve days and the christening or chrism loosening ceremony of Guthrum and his leaders was completed. Their linen head bands, placed to protect the holy oils anointed some weeks earlier at Aller, were now removed. The peace of Wedmore was agreed so Alfred held an area from Wessex to Kent whilst Guthrum held East Anglia.

Land Enclosures

The Enclosure Acts of the 18th and 19th centuries changed the countryside. On the moors they enabled drainage and access, altering farming and extending the period of use.

The changes can be seen from events at Wedmore and surrounding lands. The Bishops and Deans of Wells had owned Wedmore, having been granted the Royal Estate in 1065. After the reformation, the lands passed to Edward Seymour but after his execution in 1552 were sold to Sir Thomas Gresham, who sold it in lots. By 1770 the old estate was owned by 17 people.

The moors were areas of undrained common grazing. Their owners granted grazing rights to smallholders or commoners for a given number of cattle, sheep, geese etc. The Enclosure Awards allocated fields to each commoner in lieu of his rights. As they often used many moors commoners obtained small fields in various places. 586 acres of Wedmore Moor, to the east of the Isle of Wedmore, were included in an Enclosure Act in 1778. 258 land awards were made to 166 people. 34 acres were sold to pay lawyers, surveyors and men who dug the lattice work of rhynes and ditches,

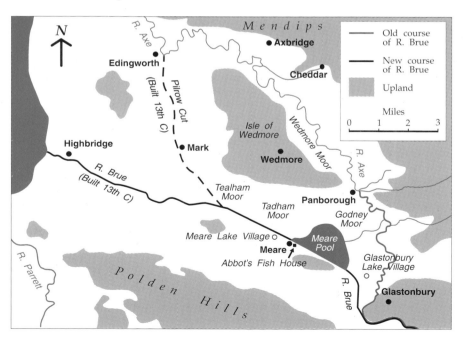

The Abbot's Fish House, Meare.

Meare Pool was to the lower left of the picture. The Abbot's Fish House, seen near the centre, would have adjoined the Pool.

built sluices, access droves and bridges. Other Acts enclosed Tealham, Tadham and Godney Moors and by 1800 nearly 10,000 acres near Wedmore had been enclosed

Meare

The conditions in medieval times would have made a journey from Wedmore to Westhay or Meare, about 3 miles away impossible. Early man would have made the journey on raised wooden trackways built across the marshes. To ease

movement and reduce floods the monks diverted the River Brue which had run from Glastonbury into the River Axe north of the Isle of Wedmore. The new river system built between 1230 and 1250 ran westwards through Meare Pool and south of the Isle of Wedmore to the sea. Even in 1765 the Sexton of Meare Church was paid to carry the church clock from Glastonbury by boat. A modern link between Wedmore and Meare had to wait until the Turnpike Roads were built in 1827.

The Abbots of Glastonbury used the Manor House at Meare as a summer

residence. Built in the early 1300's and improved in the 16th century, it is now a farmhouse and overlooks the site of Meare Pool. This lake was about 5 miles round and was used by the Abbots for fishing. Swans, herons and wildfowl were kept. A 14th century Fish House, built as a home for the chief fisherman and to cure and store fish still stands as a relic of the lake which was finally drained in the 18th century. There is scant evidence, however, of the nearby Iron Age lake village, and only a few bumps in the ground are noticeable today.

12 Peat Digging

Stacking peat blocks into "ruckles" to dry — 1920's.

Since medieval times peat has been dug on the moors for fuel and animal litter. From the end of the 19th century peat has been increasingly used for horticulture. Today almost all the peat produced is used for this purpose.

Until the early 1960's traditional hand cutting methods dating from Victorian times were used. The top soil was removed and peat blocks, or "mumps", dug using a special spade. The mumps were cut into three or four 10" x 8" (25 cms x 20 cms) turves about 3 inches (7.7 cms) thick and were stacked in small "stooks" where they partially dried. The drying was completed in larger "ruckles" which could be 8 ft. (2.4 metres) high and 4 ft. (1.2 metres) in diameter.

Today peat is excavated by mechanical means. Purpose-built machines excavate peat, cut it into blocks and automatically stack it into rows. The blocks are still hand spaced and turned to aid drying. This forms a distinctive feature in the flat countryside. After excavation and drying the peat is stockpiled before being taken to works for milling and bagging. This sedge peat is often blended with imported sphagnum moss peat because local supplies have been exhausted

Modern peat cutter which also stacks the blocks.

Peat working is permitted over an area of about 3,600 acres (1500 hectares) but some of the area will not be excavated because it is protected for nature conservation or archaeological reasons. The extraction area is mainly confined to two zones, one based upon Shapwick and Meare Heaths, and the other on Westhay Moor. About 20% of the peat excavated in the United Kingdom comes from Somerset.

Areas where peat has been extracted are providing opportunities for creative conservation that provide wildlife habitats. The Somerset Trust for Nature Conservation has created areas of reed beds, open water and wet peaty heathlands.

The peat working area forms a distinctive pattern when seen from the air.

Westhay Moor Nature Reserve — created from derelict peat workings by the Somerset Trust for Nature Conservation.

35

13 Historic Churches

North Curry Church.

The Abbey ruins at Glastonbury remind us of the once powerful Benedictine Monastery, perhaps the most famous in England, which owned and influenced much of the wetlands. Glastonbury continues to be the most venerable Christian shrine in the county but perhaps Somerset's finest architectural qualities are the perpendicular style Parish Churches with their commanding towers. The towers are an ever present feature particularly in the southern and central parts of the moors. Most date from a period of prosperity, religious revival and competition between parishes in the late 15th century to mid-16th century.

There are some 50 towers in the Levels and Moors; their height, number of window tiers and design of windows, bell openings and pinnacles depended on available money. Isle Abbots, Huish Episcopi, Long Sutton, Muchelney, Mark and Westonzoyland are a selected few from an exhaustive list. An octagonal tower dominates North Curry Church which is sometimes called the Cathedral of the Moors.

St Mary's, Isle Abbots, is notable for its architecture and history. Niches in the tower still contain statues, and the south porch has a fan vaulted roof. Its bright, peaceful interior and its furnishings are synonymous with the story of the English church.

The distinctive 15th century tower of St Mary's, Westonzoyland, stands

The distinctive tower of Westonzoyland Church.

Abbey ruins at Glastonbury.

out for miles across the moors. It has one of the finest naves in Somerset, the roof having large tie beams with carved angels and bosses. An elegantly restored rood screen has a rood loft which is an example of what has been lost from many churches. On a buttress and a bench end are the initials of Richard Bere, the last but one Abbot of Glastonbury, indicating the monastery's involvement in the development of the Parish Church. Initials of Abbots are also at Chedzoy, Othery, Ashcott, High Ham, East Brent and Meare. Westonzoyland's records tell that the bells were rung in thanksgiving after the Battle of Sedgemoor 1685.

The craftsmanship of Somerset's carvers abounds. Long Sutton's fan vaulted screen, roof and Jacobean pulpit are spectacular with colour; other Jacobean pulpits are at Huish Episcopi and Mark which has carved corbels of Kings, Queens and Clergy. Carved bench ends show a little of medieval life and in the Churches of East Lyng, East Brent and Brent Knoll are depicted the pelican, sheep, geese, a stag, goat, butterflies, teasels, wrestlers, a miller, a woodcutter, flowers, a courting couple and biblical scenes. The initials of Mary Tudor are at Chedzoy but three fascinating ends at Brent Knoll tell

the story of the downfall and execution of a fox. They are thought to represent the local unpopularity of Bishop Fox, Bishop of Bath and Wells 1490 - 1492 because of his purchases of land in the area.

The small Norman church of St Peter's Catcott has an unspoilt charm. Its pews are slotted to allow childrens stools to be pulled into the passageway and a 17th Century gallery has open flat balustrading. An historic wall text reminds women to be sober, chaste, keepers of home and to love their husbands.

The Quaker Meeting House at Long Sutton built in 1717 is simple and well proportioned. It has plain scrubbed benches and a tranquil atmosphere.

The Jacobean pulpit at Long Sutton Church.

The three satirical bench ends in Brent Knoll Church.

14 The Future

Our natural resources and historic features and buildings are fortunately well appreciated. Ways are being found to protect the landscape and the wildlife habitats, conserve historic sites and buildings and promote interpretation facilities.

In the past, changes to the landscape and countryside have been slow and man has co-existed with nature, sharing the habitats of birds, plants, trees and insects. Technical advances in agriculture and engineering mean that it is easier to drain and dramatically change the wetland scenery. Developments and visitor pressures caused by increased mobility and prosperity could also harm the area. They need to be planned for and designed sympathetically.

Government, Local Authorities, Trusts and other bodies are becoming involved. The Levels and Moors are acknowledged to be an area where the natural beauty should be conserved and enhanced. Arrangements can be agreed with landowners over much of the area for the management of land in a sensitive way. These set a pattern of grazing and haycutting but finance from official sources is essential. The wet conditions of the pastures are dependent on water level controls in the main rhynes and ditches which

are in the hands of statutory bodies. Their co-operation and that of government and the farming industry are important factors for achieving acceptable livelihoods for farmers and the protection of wildlife.

Reserves declared by Government and managed by English Nature; those of the Royal Society for the Protection of Birds, the Somerset Trust for Nature Conservation and other bodies plus the creation of nature areas and open water by landowners are developing ranges of

habitats. Facilities for people to enjoy these areas need to be controlled and timed to prevent disturbance. Disused peat workings provide many opportunities, however the degree of risks to the interests of the Levels and Moors are dependent on the willingness and enthusiasm of those who are ultimately responsible. Continued efforts towards the complete understanding of this wetland will help the essential co-operation and actions needed for its conservation.

15 Places to Visit

Visitor Centres and Museums

The Willows and Wetlands Visitor Centre, Meare Green, Stoke St Gregory.

The Levels Farm Visitor Centre, New Road Farm, East Huntspill.

The Peat Moors Visitor Centre, Willows Peat Co. Garden Centre, Westhay.

The County Museum, Taunton Castle.

Somerset Rural Life Museum, Glastonbury.

Admiral Blake Museum, Blake Street, Bridgwater.

The Tribunal Museum, High Street, Glastonbury.

The Ashmolean Museum, Oxford - contains The Alfred Jewel.

Historic Sites and Buildings

Muchelney - Abbey, The Priest's House, Parish Church and medieval buildings.

Midelney Manor - Medieval Manor House and heronry.

Meare - Medieval Abbot's Fish House and Manor House.

Glastonbury - Abbey ruins and historic town.

Prehistoric Trackway reconstructions at Shapwick Heath Nature Reserve and Godwins Peat Works near Burtle.

Parish Churches - particularly Westonzoyland, Isle Abbots, Huish Episcopi, Long Sutton, North Curry, Catcott and Brent Knoll.

Wildlife Reserves

Visits are necessarily within limits or require permission:-

Somerset Trust for Nature Conservation Reserves at Westhay Moor.

Nature Conservancy Council Reserves - Shapwick Heath and Bridgwater Bay.

Royal Society for the Protection of Birds. Reserves at Swell Hill, Fivehead and West Sedgemoor.

Features, Viewing Points and places of interest

Glastonbury Tor (520 ft AOD) and Brent Knoll (440 ft AOD).

Burrow Mump, Burrowbridge and nearby site of Athelney Abbey.

Red Hill, near Curry Rivel - to view West Sedgemoor and Southlake Moor.

Walton Hill (south of Street) overlooking Butleigh Moor and Kings Sedgemoor.

Turn Hill (between High Ham and Aller) overlooking Kings Sedgemoor.

Moorlinch Church and Churchyard - overlooking Kings Sedgemoor and site of Battle of Sedgemoor 1685.

Axbridge Bypass Layby, NW of Axbridge - looking south over Levels and Moors.

The British Water Zoo, Cliff Street, Cheddar.

The English Basket Centre, Curload, near Burrowbridge.

Westonzoyland Pumping Station, near Burrowbridge.

The Burton Pynsent Monument, near Curry Rivel and the Admiral Hood Monument, near Compton Dundon.

Circular Walks - Willows and Wetlands Visitor Centre, North Curry and River Tone.

Glastonbury Tor.

16　Further Reading

History and Events

The Archaeology of Somerset, M Aston and I Burrow, SCC 1982.

Prehistory of the Somerset Levels, J M Coles and B J Orme. Somerset Levels Project 1989.

The Lake Villages of Somerset, Arthur Bulleid, Glastonbury Antiquarian Society (7th Edition 1980).

A History of Somerset, Robert Dunning, Darwen County History Series, Phillimoor 1983.

History of Somerset, R W Dunning, SCC 1987.

Alfred of Athelney - Alfred the Great, J Pelling in the History First Series, Cambridge University Press 1977.

Arthur, The King in the West, R W Dunning, Alan Sutton, St Martin Press 1988.

The Monmouth Rebellion, R W Dunning, Dovecote Press 1984.

A History of Wedmore, F J Pearce, 1971.

Drainage

Drainage of the Somerset Levels, M Williams, Cambridge University Press 1970.

Landscape, Scenery and Wildlife

The Making of the English Landscape - The Somerset Landscape, Michael Havinden, Hodder and Stoughton 1981.

Sedgemoor, Its History and Natural History - Bernard Storer, Dovecote Press 1985.

Wildlife of the Somerset Levels and Moors, Stan Davies and Rob Jarman, RSPB.

The Willows of the British Isles, Theresa Brendell, Shire Natural History Series 1985.

The Lapwing, Peter Weaver, Shire Natural History Series 1987.

Where to Watch Birds in Somerset, Avon, Gloucestershire and Wiltshire, Ken Hull and John Govett, Christopher Helm 1988.

The Field Guide Series of Books for Nature Lovers - Readers Digest Association, published during 1980's.

Willow and Peat Industry

Baskets and Basketmaking. Alastair Heseltine, Shire Publications 1982.

The Story of Peat, A Brief Guide - Willow Peat Co, Westhay 1988.

Peat Local Plan, County Planning Officer, SCC 1989.

Historic Churches

The Buildings of England, South and West Somerset, Nikolaus Pevsner, Penguin 1958.

Church of Somerset, A K Wickham, David and Charles 1965.

The Rural Bench Ends of Somerset, Peter Poyntz-Wright, Avebury 1983.

Christianity in Somerset, Robert W Dunning, SCC 1976.

Cleeve and Muchelney Abbeys. A Handbook for Teachers, Sue Watling, English Heritage 1989.

Churches in South Somerset. Two selected Church Tours, Leaflet by Leisure and Recreation Officer, South Somerset DC.

General

Somerset Levels and Moors Strategy, Framework for Implementation, County Planning Officer, SCC 1984.

Somerset Levels and Moors, Consultation Report of Survey, County Planning Officer, SCC 1981.

Avalon and Sedgemoor, Desmond Wilcox, Tabb House republished 1989.

Shire County Guide Somerset, Martyn Brown, Shire Publications 1988.

Somerset, A Portrait in Colour, Julian Cornice and Robert Bush, Dovecote Press 1989.

Wetland Life in the Somerset Levels, Patrick Sutherland and Adam Nicholson, Michael Joseph 1986.

The SCC Local History Library, The Castle, Taunton, contains many of the above plus other records and publications about the area.